Dinosaurs, Popcorn, Penguins & More
ACTIVITY BOOK

by Donna Whyte

Crystal Springs
BOOKS
A division of **SDE** Staff Development for Educators

Peterborough, New Hampshire

Published by Crystal Springs Books
A division of Staff Development for Educators (SDE)
75 Jaffrey Road, PO Box 500
Peterborough, NH 03458
1-800-321-0401
www.crystalsprings.com
www.sde.com

© 2004 Crystal Springs Books
Published 2004
Printed in the United States of America

08 07 06 05 04   2 3 4 5

ISBN: 1-884548-68-7

Art Director, Designer, and Production Coordinator: Soosen Dunholter
Illustrations by Joyce Orchard Garamella: front and back covers, and
pages 1, 3, 7, 17, 20, 30, 38, 50, 59, 66, 72, 78, 88, 97, 104, 114, and 122
All other illustrations by Marci McAdam

Dedication

This book is dedicated to the children and teachers who sing along with me. Each reminds me of the magic music holds in learning.

Acknowledgments

Many thanks to Sandy Taylor and Soosen Dunholter for their hard work keeping this project moving, and to Joyce Orchard Garamella and Marci McAdam, whose illustrations so vividly represent my thoughts. And finally, thank you, Taylor Whyte and Victoria Mawdesley, for your great ideas!

Contents

Introduction

Dinosaurs, Popcorn, Penguins & More Activity Book offers a variety of practical, easy-to-use, and fun activities that will bring music and learning to your classroom. The book is divided into 15 sections, one for each of the thematic songs. The activities were created to extend, enrich, and practice the basic learning concepts that each song presents. Also included are reproducible masters to help you bring these engaging activities to your students more easily. It is my hope that the power of music will add motivation and enjoyment to your classroom learning experiences.

1. The Dinosaur Stomp

CHORUS:
Stomp, Stomp, Stomp,
Do the Dinosaur Stomp!
Stomp, Stomp, Stomp,
Do the Dino Stomp.

Dinosaurs, they roamed the Earth,
So many years ago.
I want to know what happened.
I really want to know.
What did they eat each day?
How'd they get around?
We've learned about these guys
From fossils in the ground.
We know some were gigantic.
So many different types!
Some were not so big.
Some even had some stripes.

CHORUS

Tyrannosaurus was big and bold.
T. rex was so mean.
A giant head and big, huge teeth,
Eyes that were so keen.
Triceratops you know
By the three horns on his head.
He walked on all four legs
And lived out on the edge.
Brontosaurus was humongous.
He loved to eat the leaves.
His long neck stretched way up there,
To reach the tops of trees.

CHORUS repeats 2 times

Pterodactyl, the flying dino,
With the pointy head and beak—
I'll bet you didn't know
This dino had no teeth.
Stegosaurus was a dinosaur
With scales all down his back.
His tail was his weapon,
SMACK, CRACK, WHACK!
The dinosaurs that ate green plants
Are called the herbivores.
Some dinos chowed down meat—
They're the carnivores.

CHORUS repeats 2 times

Dinosaurs in the water,
On the land and in the sky,
Now they're labeled *gone, extinct*,
Do you wonder why?

CHORUS repeats 4 times

Dinosaur Stompers

MATERIALS:

- 2 one-pound coffee cans for each child
- awl or screwdriver
- hammer
- 2 lengths of nylon or cotton rope for each child (lengths depend on height of each child)
- colored construction paper
- sheets of white paper (long enough to wrap around cans)

To make a pair of stompers, punch a hole in one side of a coffee can approximately 2 inches down from the top rim. Punch another hole directly across from the first one, also about 2 inches down from the top rim. Repeat with the second can (and with as many other pairs of cans as you will need for your students). Thread one end of the rope through one hole and tie the end firmly with a knot. Thread the other end of the rope through the other hole and knot securely. Repeat with the other can. Be sure to allow enough rope so that the child can stand upright on the cans and hold onto a rope in either hand. Using the construction paper, cut out foot shapes similar to those in the illustration, or make up your own design—just be sure it is larger than the diameter of the can. Give each child a pair of stompers, a pair of foot shapes, and two sheets of white paper. Tell them to decorate the sheets of paper and then wrap each sheet around each stomper, taping it in place. Next, have them tape a foot shape to the bottom of each stomper. Tell the children to stand on top of their stompers while holding onto the attached ropes, and do the Dinosaur Stomp.

Consider This

A quick and easy alternative is to use large-size empty Kleenex boxes instead of coffee cans for the dinosaur feet. The kids simply slip their feet inside the boxes (without shoes on) and do the stomp.

Favorite Dinosaur Graph

Display the pictures of the dinosaurs and ask the children to pick their favorites. Use a bar graph to illustrate the children's responses. Then ask them questions, such as:

    a. Which dinosaur was chosen the "most"?
    b. Which was chosen the "least"?
    c. How many more votes did _____ receive than _____?
    d. What was the second favorite dinosaur?

MATERIALS:

- pictures or illustrations of 5 different dinosaurs: T. rex, stegosaurus, triceratops, pterodactyl, and brontosaurus (see page 10)

Have the kids use books, videos, and the Internet to research dinosaurs of their choice. Then have them report their findings to the class.

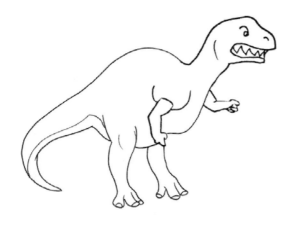

T. REX

STEGOSAURUS

TRICERATOPS

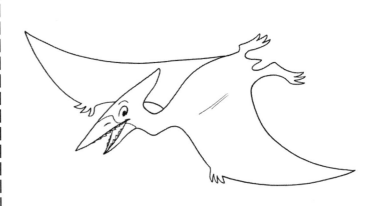

PTERODACTYL

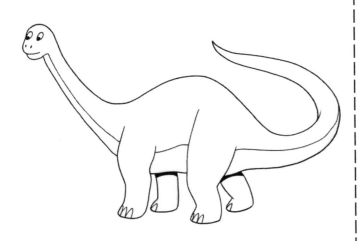

BRONTOSAURUS

OTHER

Footprint Predictions

MATERIALS:
- butcher paper

Draw a dinosaur track measuring approximately 24"x18" on butcher paper and make duplicates for the class. Ask the children to estimate how many of their footprints would fit into the track. Divide the children into teams, give each team a copy of the track, and tell each team to trace one child's foot onto the team's track print. Tell them to think of what they can do to get as many feet as possible into the track. After the teams have finished, compare the number of kid footprints inside each dinosaur track and the methods used for tracing as many feet as they could fit.

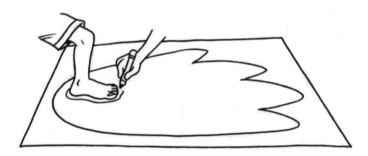

"Me"-saurus

MATERIALS:
- "Dinosaur Description" (see page 12)

Ask the children to draw a picture of a new dinosaur they've imagined in their minds. Tell them it's fun to combine their own names with part of a dinosaur's name, such as "Cartersaurus" or "Taylordactyl." Once the kids have finished their sheets, hang them around the classroom so that everyone can see the different kinds of "Me"-sauruses.

DINOSAUR DESCRIPTION

Name of your new dinosaur:

_____

Draw a picture of your dinosaur.

What does your dinosaur like to do?

_____

_____

What does your dinosaur like to eat?

_____

_____

If a friend had to babysit your dinosaur, what would the babysitter need to know?

_____

_____

Dinosaur Fossil

Roll the play dough into a ball and press it into a 3"-diameter circle. Place the strip snugly around the dough and staple it in place. Choose a dinosaur, lay it on its side in the dough, and press down. Then carefully remove the dinosaur so that its impression is left in the dough. Mix the plaster of paris according to package directions and pour ¾ cup into the impression and over the rest of the dough circle. Let the plaster dry overnight, or according to package directions. Remove the strip and peel off the play dough to reveal the dinosaur fossil.

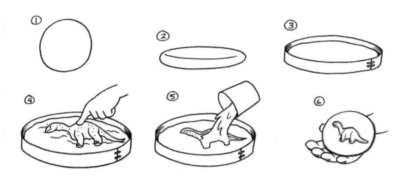

Homemade Play Dough

1 cup flour
½ cup salt
2 tablespoons vegetable oil
1 teaspoon alum (available at drugstores)
food coloring

Combine the flour, salt, oil, and alum in a small bowl and mix well. Stir in a small amount of water at a time until the mixture has the consistency of bread dough. Add a drop or two of food coloring and knead until the color is well blended. Makes about 1½ cups.

MATERIALS:

- ½ cup play dough for each child (homemade works best, see below)
- 12"x2" strip of oak tag or poster paper for each child
- small plastic dinosaurs, 1 for each child (sold at science shops and dollar stores)
- plaster of paris (sold at hardware and craft stores)

Consider This

Instead of using a dinosaur, you can make tracks in the play dough and then a plaster cast of the tracks.

Dinosaurs: Fact or Fiction?

Divide the children into two teams and have them form two lines. Shuffle the fact/fiction cards, place them in a stack face side down, and turn over the first card. Read the statement on the card and ask the first child in one line whether she thinks the statement is true or false and to call out her answer. If she is correct, her team gets a point. If her answer is incorrect, the other team must restate the sentence correctly to get the point. For example, if the statement is "Dinosaurs ate tacos," the other team must restate it correctly, as in "Dinosaurs did not eat tacos." Another, more challenging way to play this game is to have the two teams come up with their own fact/fiction statements, based on what they have learned in class about dinosaurs. Suggest that they include statements that trick the other team into thinking that something is correct when it isn't, and vice versa.

DINOSAUR FACT/FICTION CARDS

Dinosaurs played soccer.	Dinosaurs lived in the sea.	Dinosaurs had long necks.
Dinosaurs fought with swords.	Dinosaurs had no teeth.	Pterodactyls used their tails as weapons.
Stegosauruses had scales down their backs.	All dinosaurs are extinct.	Dinosaurs lived in igloos.

DINOSAUR FACT/FICTION CARDS

Dinosaurs lived at the edge of the forest.	Dinosaurs walked on two legs.	Dinosaurs walked on four legs.
Dinosaurs had big teeth.	Dinosaurs ate tacos.	Dinosaurs flew.
Dinosaurs were all huge.	Dinosaurs ate meat.	Dinosaurs ate leaves.

2. Paint on Your Easel

Tune: "Pop Goes the Weasel"

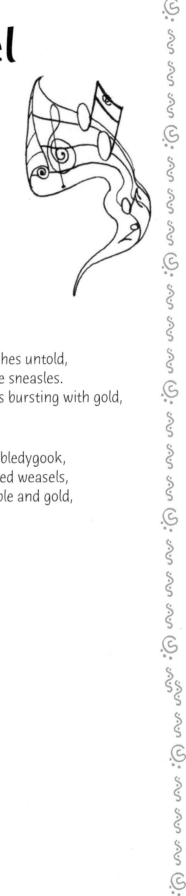

Take a pound of gobbledygook
And three nearsighted weasels!
Mix 'em all with purple and gold,
Paint on your easel.

A frog with ham and cheese on a roll,
A turkey with the measles,
A bucket full of silver and gold,
Paint on your easel.

CHORUS:
Imagination up to the moon,
Creative and so dreamful.
Make it be whatever you choose,
Paint on your easel.

Stars and suns and comets and moons,
Up in the sky so peaceful,
Let them know you want them to be
Paint on your easel.

CHORUS

Lollipops the hummingbird brings,
To Mr. and Mrs. Geesel.
Their house is red.
Their trees are all blue.
Paint on your easel.

CHORUS

A pirate ship has riches untold,
But Captain's got the sneasles.
The treasure chest is bursting with gold,
Paint on your easel.

Take a pound of gobbledygook,
And three nearsighted weasels,
Mix 'em all with purple and gold,
Paint on your easel.

Imagination Easel

MATERIALS:
- drawing paper

Discuss the song "Paint on Your Easel," and ask the children what they think the word *gobbledygook* might mean. Have them brainstorm things that take imagination. Next, tell them to close their eyes and use their imaginations to travel to a place where they have never been or to picture something totally imaginary. Tell them to draw what they imagined, using a lot of detail and color to help others envision what they saw in their imaginations.

If a child needs help, remind him of parts of the song, such as:

- a frog holding a ham and cheese sandwich on a roll
- a nearsighted weasel
- a turkey with the measles
- stars, suns, comets, moons
- a treasure chest
- a pirate ship
- lollipops carried by hummingbirds

Imagination Wand

MATERIALS:
- craft sticks
- glitter
- curly ribbon of multiple colors

Tell the children to use their imaginations to create their own imagination wands. Then have them test their wands by imagining they are something or somewhere else—in the ocean, for example. Tell them to wave their wands and act out their scenarios, using their imaginations.

Imagine If …

Model for the class some examples of good imagination questions and discuss how those questions can sometimes sound silly. For example, "Imagine if planes rode around on streets … or if dogs walked on two feet … or if kids were in charge at your house.…" Divide the children into pairs or groups and ask each group to come up with two questions that their classmates would have to use their imaginations to answer. Have each group write its questions on separate slips of paper. Ask the children to trade slips with other groups and to illustrate what the answers to the questions might look like.

MATERIALS:
• drawing paper
• keen imaginations

Imagination Storyboard

For this teacher-directed activity, model a familiar story before making one up with the children. Begin by writing "Who," "Where," "What," and "Why" on the blackboard or overhead. Using "Goldilocks and the Three Bears" as an example, ask who the main characters are in that story and write down the names as the children say them. Do the same with "Where," "What," and "Why." Once the children understand the procedure, act as the scribe for the classroom story by asking the same questions and writing down the children's responses.

MATERIALS:
none

3. Opposites

Tune: "Camptown Races"

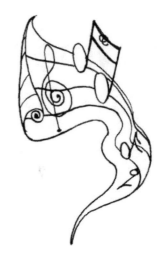

The opposite of hot is cold. Doo-Dah.
   Doo-Dah.
The opposite of young is old. All Doo-Dah
   Day.
Hot and cold, young and old,
Opposites are fun to find, all Doo-Dah Day.

The opposite of short is tall. Doo-Dah.
   Doo-Dah.
The opposite of big is small. All Doo-Dah
   Day.
Short and tall, big and small,
Opposites are fun to find, all Doo-Dah Day.

The opposite of right is wrong. Doo-Dah.
   Doo-Dah.
The opposite of weak is strong. All Doo-
   Dah Day.
Right and wrong, weak and strong,
Opposites are fun to find, all Doo-Dah Day.

The opposite of black is white. Doo-Dah.
   Doo-Dah.
The opposite of day is night. All Doo-Dah
   Day.
Black and white, day and night,
Opposites are fun to find, all Doo-Dah Day.

The opposite of false is true. Doo-Dah.
   Doo-Dah.
The opposite of used is new. All Doo-Dah
   Day.
False and true, used and new,
Opposites are fun to find, all Doo-Dah Day.

The opposite of thick is thin. Doo-Dah.
   Doo-Dah.
The opposite of lose is win. All Doo-Dah Day.
Thick and thin, lose and win,
Opposites are fun to find, all Doo-Dah Day.

The opposite of stop is go. Doo-Dah.
   Doo-Dah.
The opposite of high is low. All Doo-Dah Day.
Stop and go, high and low,
Opposites are fun to find, all Doo-Dah Day.

The opposite of yes is no. Doo-Dah.
   Doo-Dah.
The opposite of shrink is grow. All Doo-Dah
   Day.
Yes and no, shrink and grow,
Opposites are fun to find, all Doo-Dah Day.

The opposite of in is out. Doo-Dah.
   Doo-Dah.
The opposite of whisper is shout. All Doo-Dah
   Day.
In and out, whisper and shout,
Opposites are fun to find, all Doo-Dah Day.

Opposites Flip Book

Make a flip book for each child based on the number of opposites you want to include (there are 18 pairs in the song). Fold the sheets in half crosswise (hamburger style), bind them along the folded edge, and then cut each page in half, creating two flaps side by side (see illustration). Make copies of the reproducible, cut out each word/picture, and glue one to each flap, making sure to put opposite words on opposite flaps but not directly across from each other. Have the children pick a word and then flip through the other side to find its opposite.

Opposites Story

Share the story with the children. Then ask whether they can identify any of the opposites in the story. Highlight and number the pairs of opposites for the class as the kids find them.

MATERIALS:

• 8½"x11" sheets of paper

• "Opposites" reproducible (see pages 22-24)

MATERIALS:

• "Opposites Story" (see page 25), or make up your own

• highlighters or highlighting tape (tape available from Crystal Springs Books)

hot	cold	short	tall
right	wrong	black	white
true	false	thick	thin

Pigs like mud.

Pigs can fly.

yes	no	young	old

big	small	weak	strong

day	night	old	new

stop	go	in	out
lose	**win**	**up**	**down**
grow	shrink	whisper	shout

OPPOSITES STORY

Once upon a time, there was an old man who lived near a small town. Each morning the man would push a cart into town. The road he traveled was short and straight. He would start out early so that he could get to the store when it opened. The old man was a kind and happy person who loved to give to others. Sometimes he gave away all the things he bought before he returned home.

Once upon a time, there was a young woman who lived far from a large town. Each evening the woman would pull a wagon into town. The road she traveled was long and winding. She would start out late and not stop so that she could arrive at the store right before it closed. The young woman was cruel and sad. Sometimes she took things from people's yards as she left town.

Memory Game

MATERIALS:
• "Opposites" reproducible (see pages 22–24)
• "Other Opposites" (see page 27)

Photocopy the reproducible, cut it into separate cards, and place all the cards face side down on the floor or a tabletop. Have children take turns flipping over two cards as they try to locate two words that are opposites of each other, such as *hot* and *cold*. If a student finds a pair, she takes the two cards and turns over two more. If they too match as opposites, she continues to turn over pairs of cards. When she fails to get a match, she turns those two cards back over, face side down, and the next child takes a turn. The game continues in the same fashion until all the cards have been matched. The child with the most pairs of opposites wins the game. Extend the game by substituting the words on the Other Opposites sheet.

Consider This

Turn this into a game that is played like "Old Maid" but uses an "Old Mr. _____" card. Put a digital photo of Old Mr. _____ on a card matching the opposites cards, shuffle the deck, pass out the cards, and have the kids lay down any pairs they may have. Then they take turns picking a card from another kid's hand, trying to find a match. The game ends when all the cards are gone. The child with the most pairs wins; the child with the Old Mr. _____ card loses the game.

OTHER OPPOSITES

come — go	fast — slow
first — last	present — past
warm — cool	kind — cruel
quick — slow	hide — show
far — near	cloudy — clear
dark — light	dull — bright
up — down	smile — frown
finish — start	whole — part
dirty — clean	fat — lean
float — sink	stretch — shrink
good — bad	happy — sad
push — pull	empty — full
bold — shy	laugh — cry
open — close	comes — goes
rich — poor	less — more
sour — sweet	messy — neat
curly — straight	early — late
to — from	all — some
give — take	asleep — awake

Opposites Game

To start the game, have all the children stand behind their chairs. Tell them that you are going to call out a direction and that they must do the opposite of whatever you say. For example, if you say, "Stand up," the children should sit down. If you say, "Frown," they should smile. If you say, "Laugh," they should pretend to cry, and so on.

Consider This

Pass out index cards with opposites written on them. Ask each kid to illustrate what his opposite would look like and then find his partner.

Opposites Wheel

Have each child stack her two plates together and pierce a hole through their centers, using a mathematical compass, an awl, or something similar. Ask each child to cut a rectangular shape out of the top plate and then write 10 words, equally spaced, around the center of that plate (see illustration). On the bottom plate, have each child write 10 opposite words and space them equally around the outer edge. Point out that these words should be written so that they will show through the top plate's rectangular cutout when the two plates are stacked together (see illustration). Now have each child put her plates together again so that the top one has the cutout, and connect them with the brass fastener through the center hole. Ask each child to pick a word on the top plate and then turn it until she finds its opposite on the bottom plate.

MATERIALS:

- white paper plates, 2 for each child
- mathematical compass, awl, or similar tool
- brass fasteners

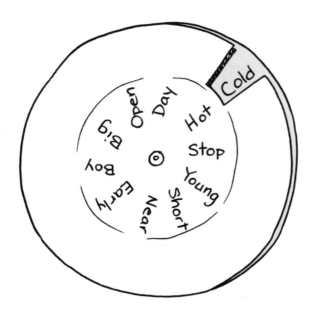

4. Your Choices Are All Up to You

Tune: Beethoven's "Ode to Joy"

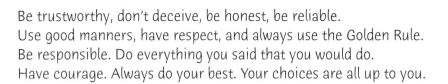

Be trustworthy, don't deceive, be honest, be reliable.
Use good manners, have respect, and always use the Golden Rule.
Be responsible. Do everything you said that you would do.
Have courage. Always do your best. Your choices are all up to you.

Show you care, be kind, forgive, help others when they have a need.
Citizens, obey the laws and rules, respect authority.
Don't deceive or cheat or steal, and do your share to help your school.
Have courage. Always do your best. Your choices are all up to you.

Take turns and share, play by the rules, use self-control and discipline.
Always think before you act, be gracious when you lose or win.
Use kind words. Your tone is important. Compromise. Be humble, too.
Have courage. Always do your best. Your choices are all up to you.

Be trustworthy, don't deceive, be honest, be reliable.
Use good manners, have respect, and always use the Golden Rule.
Be responsible. Do everything you said that you would do.
Have courage. Always do your best. Your choices are all up to you.

Character Traits Necklace

D raw an oval, circle, square, retangle, diamond, and triangle on a sheet of poster paper, and write a character trait from the song inside each one of the shapes. Make a copy of the sheet for each child. Tell the children to decorate the shapes, cut them all out, punch a hole in each one, and then string them onto a piece of yarn to wear as a necklace. As you discuss a character trait with the children, tell them the shape the word is written on; have them locate that shape on their necklaces and hold it up. This is a great way to teach shapes and character traits at the same time!

MATERIALS:

- poster paper
- 18" length of yarn for each child
- hole punch

Fan of Manners

T ell the children to cut out the pieces of the fan and to write a word or draw a picture on each piece that describes some aspect of "good manners." Words might include "Please!," "Thank you!," "I'm sorry," or "Excuse me," for example. Pictures might show someone holding the door for someone else, helping someone else carry things, and so on. Have each child stack his fan pieces together, punch a hole in one end, and place a brass fastener in the hole. Then tell the kids to spread out the pieces to create fans and show that "manners are cool."

MATERIALS:

- "Fan" reproducible (see page 32)
- hole punch
- brass fasteners

Manners are cool!

What Would You Do?

Make two columns on a piece of chart paper and label one "Good Choice" and the other "Bad Choice." Gather the children together and read a question from the What If … sheet. Have them brainstorm what they would do if they were in that situation, or what they think the right action would be. Let the children vote to determine whether the answer is a good choice or a bad choice, and write it in the appropriate column. Discuss why it is sometimes hard to make good choices and why some people may make bad choices.

Good Choice	Bad Choice
Tell the librarian the truth.	Say you never had the book.
Look for it.	Blame someone for stealing it.
Offer to replace it.	Cry.

What if I lost my library book...

MATERIALS:
- chart paper
- "What If …" sheet (see page 34)

Name Poetry

Have each child write her name vertically down the left side of a piece of paper, starting each letter about 2 inches away from the left edge of the sheet. (This space will let her add another letter or two, if necessary.) Ask the children to think about words, phrases, or sentences that describe themselves and who they are, and to try to use the letters in their names with each one. For example, for the names "Donna" and "Mark," you might have:

Don't tease
Own your words
Neat work
New friends
Always do my best

My smile
A team player
be Responsible
Kind words

MATERIALS:

WHAT IF ...

... you find $20 on the sidewalk while you're walking into the school building?

... your parents have told you never to go to the park without an adult, but one day when your parents aren't home, a friend comes by and asks you to go to the park with her alone?

... you don't know the answer to a question on a test, but you can see your neighbor's paper?

... you lose your library book?

... you're in a store with no money, but no one's watching and you see that you can just take a candy bar?

... people are making fun of someone you don't know on the playground?

... you break your mom's favorite vase?

... your brother lies to your parents and you know it's a lie?

... your grandmother calls and asks you to help shovel her driveway, but you're in the middle of a video game?

... you're in the middle of a game outside and a neighbor comes over to play with you?

... you make plans with a friend to do something, but then another friend, whom you like more than the first, calls to ask you to do something else?

... your friend wants to spend time with someone you know her parents don't like, and she asks you to lie to her parents and say that she's going to your house?

Faces with Feelings

Photocopy the reproducible, cut it apart, and glue each face onto a card. Show one of the cards to the children and ask them to brainstorm what this person might be feeling and/or thinking. Ask whether it is a feeling that they have ever had. Give the children one card each and ask them to draw or write about a time when they felt the same way as the faces pictured on their cards.

MATERIALS:
• "Faces with Feelings" reproducible (see page 36)

Classroom Stationery

Draw a frame in the center of a sheet of paper to create a writing area (see illustration). Around the perimeter of the sheet, mark off a space for each child in your classroom. Pass around the sheet and ask each child to draw a picture of himself at school in one of the spaces and to include his first name. After every child has filled in one of the spaces, make photocopies of the paper to create classroom stationery that you can use for all notes home.

MATERIALS:
• 8½"x11" sheets of paper

Consider This

For special occasions, use a color copier.

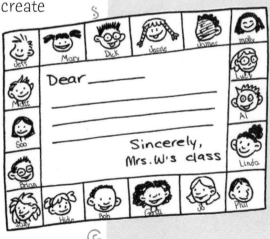

Dinosaurs, Popcorn, Penguins & More

REPRODUCIBLE PAGE

Community Quilt

Discuss with the children some of the ways in which people can be helpful to one another, and then ask each student to draw a picture, using the fabric crayons, of one of those ways on his square of paper. Tell the kids not to write words or names because they will come out backwards. Iron each child's paper square onto a fabric square. Punch a hole in each of the four corners of the square, being careful not to make them too close to the edges. Give the children their own fabric squares and have them tie their squares together with yarn to build a community quilt, which you can then hang in your classroom.

MATERIALS:
- squares of white paper, 1 for each child
- squares of white fabric, 1 for each child
- fabric crayons
- yarn
- hole punch

Consider This

a. If you don't want to use an iron, give the children fabric markers or fabric paints and have them draw directly on the white fabric squares.

b. Invite other classes to make their own community quilts, and then join them all together and hang them on a wall outside the classrooms.

5. Spring and Summer, Fall and Winter

Tune: "Battle Hymn of the Republic"

CHORUS:
Spring and summer, fall and winter,
Spring and summer, fall and winter,
Spring and summer, fall and winter,
Each season marches on.

Spring is the season when the flowers start to bloom.
April showers help them grow. The summer's coming soon.
The grass is turning greener as the birdies sing their tune.
Each season marches on.

CHORUS

Summer comes and school is out. We're playing in the sun.
I like to swim and splash around. I'm having so much fun.
We're going on vacation—do you think you'd like to come?
Each season marches on.

CHORUS

Fall has come; we're back to school. The leaves are turning red.
The pumpkin on the porch has got some frost upon his head.
Halloween is coming and the scarecrow's gone to bed.
Each season marches on.

CHORUS

Winter is the time for hats and coats and boots and gloves.
Snowman with a carrot nose, a top hat that he loves.
Skating on a frozen pond, a pair of turtledoves.
Each season marches on.

CHORUS repeats 2 times

Season Sticks

Make enough copies of the reproducible so that each child will have a seasonal picture. Hand them out along with the craft sticks. Have each child color her season and tape it to a craft stick. Ask the children to decide which seasons their pictures represent and to form a large circle. As the song plays, tell the children to start marching along in the circle. When each child hears her season, she moves to the middle of the circle, holds up her picture, and marches with the other kids who have pictures from the same season. Kids with different seasons continue marching in the outside circle. When the next season plays, the children inside the circle move back to the outer circle, and children holding the new season move into the center and repeat the same sequence.

MATERIALS:

- "Seasons" reproducible (see page 40)
- large craft sticks
- *Dinosaurs, Popcorn, Penguins & More* CD

A Tree of All Seasons

Tell the children to fold their pieces of paper into quarters, creating four boxes in which to draw. Have them keep their papers folded like a book, with the folded edges on the left side and at the top. Tell them to write the name of the current season at the bottom of the first box (or page). Have them look at a real tree near your classroom and draw what the tree looks like. If there are no trees, provide each child with a photocopied page from a book that shows a tree from the current season (see recommendations below) and have the kids draw that tree. When they have finished drawing, tell them to write their names on the front of their books. Collect all the books, store them away, and bring them out when the next season has changed the appearance of the tree (or provide photocopies of a tree from the next season). Repeat for each season. One possible schedule would be to draw a tree in October (fall), December or January (winter), April (spring), and June (summer). This school-year-long project illustrates the actual changes in the tree/season through the drawings of the children. If you ask the children to write a few words or a sentence about their drawings, you will also see developmental changes in their writing with the passage of time (the seasons)!

MATERIALS:

- 11"x14" paper, 1 sheet for each child

- real tree or a book about trees*

Consider This

Compare the changes in the kids' appearance throughout the year by taking a photo of each one while she draws her tree. Write two or three things that the child has recently learned on the back of each photo, to illustrate the "seasons of change" in what the kids have learned over time.

*I recommend either of the following:
A Tree for All Seasons (photographs) by Robin Bernard
The Seasons of Arnold's Apple Tree (illustrations) by Gail Gibbons

MATERIALS:

- "Favorite Seasons" graph (see page 43)

MATERIALS:

- construction paper of different colors
- glyph patterns for the seasons (see pages 45 and 47)
- glyph keys (see pages 44 and 46)

Graphing Our Favorite Seasons

Tell the children to fill in their copies of the graph and then pass them in to you. With younger children or to simplify the activity, you may prefer to reproduce the graph on a large sheet of paper and hang it where all can see and reach it. Ask 10 of the children to come forward one by one and color a box in the column that lists each child's favorite season. Continue with the rest of the graph as a whole-group activity, either filling it in yourself or inviting individual children to come forward to fill in or color the blanks as the class discusses them.

Glyphs for All Seasons

Glyphs are visual representations or symbols that provide information about something in a nonverbal way. Before having your children do this activity, be sure you model first how glyphs work, using something other than the seasons. Then give each child some construction paper, glyph patterns for one of the seasons, and the corresponding glyph key. Ask the children to draw, color, and/or cut out the patterns for their seasons. Now have the children construct their glyphs so that they provide information about themselves.

FAVORITE SEASONS

Name _____

Ask 10 friends to name their favorite season and record the results on the graph by coloring a box to represent each person's answer.

	Spring	Summer	Fall	Winter
10				
9				
8				
7				
6				
5				
4				
3				
2				
1				

How many people chose:

Spring _____   Summer _____   Fall _____   Winter _____

Which season was chosen most? _____

Which season was chosen least? _____

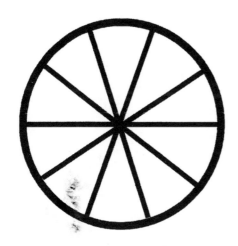

Color a piece of pie to represent each vote for the season by using the following colors. (Be sure to keep the same colors next to each other in the pie.)

Spring - Green   Summer - Yellow

Fall - Orange   Winter - Blue

GLYPH KEYS

FALL GLYPH ~ PUMPKIN

number of ridges on pumpkin = number of people who live in your house

stem shape = boy or girl

      curved stem = girl   straight stem = boy

stem color = your eye color

eye shape = color of your hair

      triangle = brown   square = red
      circle = blond   diamond = black

mouth shape = your favorite fruit

      toothless mouth = banana
      mouth with teeth on top = apple
      mouth with teeth on bottom = grapes
      mouth with teeth on top and bottom = _____

pumpkin shape = the Halloween book you like best

      tall pumpkin = *13 Nights of Halloween* by Rebecca Dickinson or
      _____(book of your choice)
      short pumpkin = *In a Dark, Dark Wood* by David A. Carter or
      _____(book of your choice)

WINTER GLYPH ~ MITTEN

color of mitten = your favorite color

thumb on the right = you are left-handed
thumb on the left = you are right-handed

design on cuff = your favorite winter sport

stripes = skiing   dots = ice scating
zigzags = snowboarding   wavy lines = _____

design on front of mitten = your favorite kind of pet

      star = cat   sun = dog   hearts = bird
      snowman = _____

FALL GLYPH ~ PUMPKIN

WINTER GLYPH ~ MITTEN

GLYPH KEYS

SPRING GLYPH ~ FLOWER

color of petals = your favorite color

number of petals = number of letters in your first name

butterfly = youngest child/only child
grasshopper = oldest child
ladybug = middle child

number of leaves = your favorite food

1 leaf = pizza	2 leaves = chocolate chip cookies
3 leaves = spaghetti and sauce	4 leaves = _____

SUMMER GLYPH ~ ICE CREAM AND CONE

color of ice cream = your age

brown = 5	pink= 6
green = 7	white = _____

color of cone = your favorite summertime activity

purple = bicycling	blue = swimming
yellow = cookout or picnic	orange = _____

number of scoops of ice cream = your favorite ice cream flavor

1 = chocolate	2 = vanilla
3 = strawberry	4 = _____

SPRING GLYPH ~ FLOWER

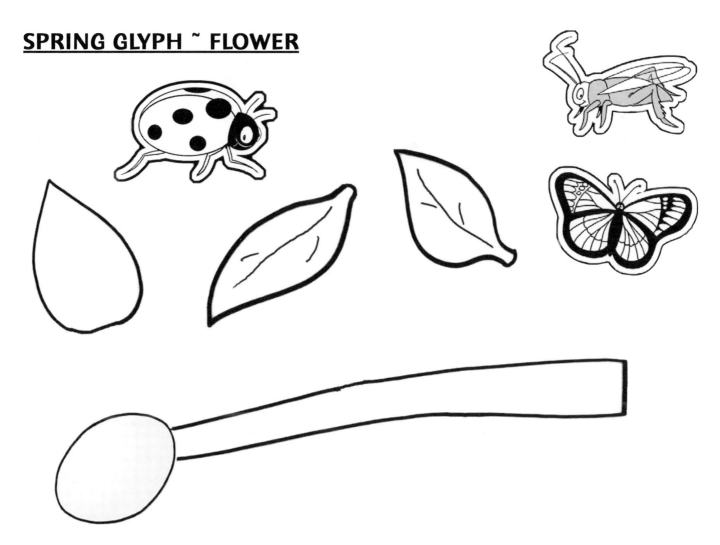

SUMMER GLYPH ~ ICE CREAM AND CONE

Sensing the Seasons

MATERIALS:

• "Sensing the Seasons" sheet (below)

Give each child four of the Sensing the Seasons sheets and have them write the name of a different season at the top of each. Tell them to stack the four sheets together and staple them along the left side to create a book. Brainstorm with the children what we can see, smell, taste, touch, and hear during each season. On the blackboard or overhead, write their responses under the appropriate season and sense. Tell the children to choose one thing from each sense that reminds them most of each season and to copy it on the corresponding line in their books. When they have finished, they will each have a booklet titled "Sensing the Seasons."

Consider This

Collect items for each season and place them in a shoe box. Smells can be re-created by placing fragrances, flavorings, or items in film containers. Ask the kids to guess the season as they examine each item in the box with eyes, ears, nose, mouth, or hands.

SENSING THE SEASONS

Seasons Wheel

Have each child stack her two plates together and pierce a hole through their centers, using a mathematical compass, awl, or something similar. Ask each child to draw lines on the bottom plate to divide it into four equal pie-shaped pieces. Then have each child draw and color a picture in each section representing one of the seasons—spring, summer, fall, and winter— making sure they are in order. (Instead of drawing, the children could use the seasonal cards on page 40.) Tell each child to cut out a pie-shaped section from the other plate that is equal to one of those on the bottom plate, but not to cut all the way to the center hole. Have each student stack her two plates so that the top one has the cutout, and fasten them together with the brass fastener. Tell each child to find her favorite season by moving the top wheel. Ask students to move their wheels forward or backward two seasons and to say which seasons they land on.

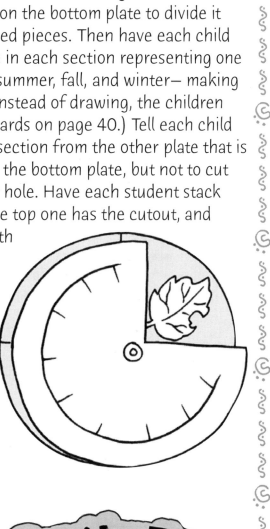

MATERIALS:
- white paper plates, 2 for each child
- mathematical compass, awl, or similar tool
- brass fasteners

Consider This

Assemble the paper-plate wheels the same way, but don't ask the children to do seasonal drawings. Instead, have each child write "Seasons of Change" on the top plate (or you can write it for her), and then glue a baby picture (or a drawing) of herself in one of the pie-shaped sections. In the next section, have each child glue in a school picture of herself from this year; then ask her to draw a picture of herself as an adult in the next section and as a senior in the last pie-shaped section.

6. Popcorn

Tune: "Shoo Fly, Don't Bother Me"

CHORUS
Popcorn, please pop for me.
Popcorn, please pop for me.
Popcorn, please pop for me.
Pop, pop, popcorn.

Tap your right foot,
Now your left foot.
Tap both those feet!
[Pop, pop, popcorn.]

Twist your waist.
Come on, do the twist.
Get your arms going!
[Pop, pop, popcorn.]

Arms up high,
Arms down low,
Arms out front.
[Pop, pop, popcorn.]

Rub your belly.
Tap your head.
Try to do both!
[Pop, pop, popcorn.]

CHORUS

Grab your right knee.
Grab your left knee.
Cross over!
[Pop, pop, popcorn.]

Jump forward.
Jump backward.
Jump up and down!
[Pop, pop, popcorn.]

Turn this way.
Turn that way.
Spin yourself around!
[Pop, pop, popcorn.]

Let's spin again,
One more time.
Are you feeling dizzy?
[Pop, pop, popcorn.]

Touch your toes.
Touch your nose.
Can you touch both?
[Pop, pop, popcorn.]

CHORUS repeats 2 times

Popcorn Percussion Instruments

Using the materials listed, let the children make a variety of percussion "instruments" to shake, rattle, and roll as they sing and move to the "Popcorn" song:

Rain sticks. Take an empty toilet paper/paper towel roll and scrunch mesh wire inside it. Pour in noisemakers of choice, cover both ends with construction paper and tape, and listen to the rhythm of the falling rain.

Maracas. Cut a slit in the bottom of a film container just large enough to insert a craft stick. Pour in noisemakers, attach the film container lid, decorate the outside, and keep the beat.

Tambourine. Decorate the back of a paper plate and then fold it in half. Pour in noisemakers, glue or staple the edges together, and strike with the hand.

Bottle shakers. Pour noisemakers into any small plastic bottle, attach the lid, decorate as desired, and shake away.

MATERIALS:

- toilet paper or paper towel rolls
- mesh wire
- paper plates
- small, clear plastic bottles
- film containers
- large craft sticks
- noisemakers (popcorn kernels, rice, beans, bells, beads, macaroni, etc.)
- construction paper
- *Dinosaurs, Popcorn, Penguins & More* CD

Popcorn Investigation

Give each child a teaspoon, a measuring cup, and a handful of popcorn kernels. Ask the children to fill out the top parts of their sheets; while they do that, you can make a batch of popcorn. After it pops, give them each a handful of the popped popcorn on a napkin or paper towel, and tell them to fill in the bottoms of their sheets. When they have finished, compare notes and eat the evidence!

MATERIALS

- "Popcorn Recording Sheet" (see page 53)
- popcorn kernels
- teaspoons and 1 cup measures
- air popper popcorn maker
- napkins or paper towels

Popcorn Sequencing

Fold the construction paper in half lengthwise (hot-dog style). Divide one side into five equal parts by drawing dotted lines from the folded side to the edge of the paper (see illustration), and give one to each child along with a copy of the reproducible. Ask the children to cut along the dotted lines on the construction paper to create five flaps or "doors" and then to number each door from 1 to 5. Have each child cut out the five pictures showing how to make popcorn and glue them in the correct order under the doors. Discuss why sequence is important in following directions, and ask the children whether a different order could produce the same result.

MATERIALS:

- large sheets of construction paper
- "Steps for Making Popcorn" reproducible (see page 54)

POPCORN RECORDING SHEET

Name _____

Before it's popped:

It feels _____

It's similar to _____

It's about the size of _____

This many pieces fit in 1 teaspoon: _____

This is what it looks like:

After it's popped:

It feels _____

It's similar to _____

It's about the size of _____

This many pieces fit in 1 cup: _____

This is what it looks like:

STEPS FOR MAKING POPCORN

Just Popped In to Hold Your Place

Ask the children to cut out their bookmarks, write their first names on them, and decorate them. Have each child paste either a picture or a drawing of himself in one of the kernels at the top. Laminate each one for durability. This makes a fun gift.

MATERIALS:

- "Popcorn Bookmark" reproducible (below)
- pictures or drawings of the students

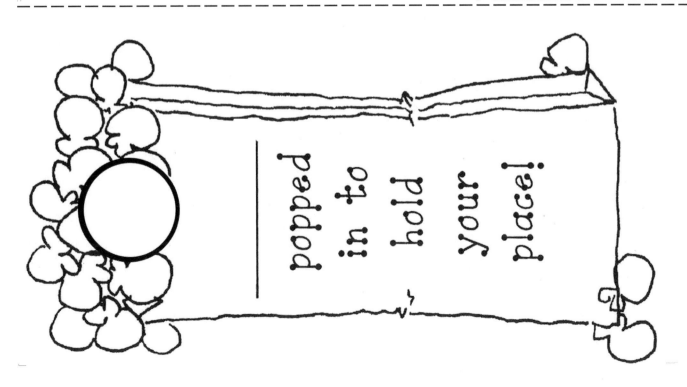

Popcorn Prediction

MATERIALS:
- popcorn kernels
- air popper popcorn maker
- measuring spoons and cups
- stop clock with minutes and seconds
- "Predictions Sheet" (see page 57)

Explain to the children that popcorn is a food that changes when it is cooked—not only in size but also in shape, color, and taste. Tell them that you want to do an experiment, and have them predict how long it will take popcorn to change. Divide the children into groups. Give each group a prediction sheet, and ask the kids to write their estimates on their sheets. Then, using a stop clock, pop some popcorn according to the groups' predictions, and have measuring cups ready to check out the results.

Pop-Corny Jokes, Riddles & Stories

MATERIALS:
- "Pop-Corny Book" reproducible (see page 58), 1 for each child

Read a book of corny jokes, tell silly riddles, and/or create goofy stories. Pass out enlarged photocopies of the reproducible and have each child cut out the two pieces and staple them together like a book. Tell the children to ask one of their parents, caregivers, or relatives to share something corny with the class by recording it in the *Pop-Corny Jokes, Riddles & Stories* book. Also ask the principal, school librarian, gym teacher, nurse, and so on to do the same. Once the pages have all come in, put them together to create a classroom book of *Pop-Corny Jokes, Riddles & Stories*.

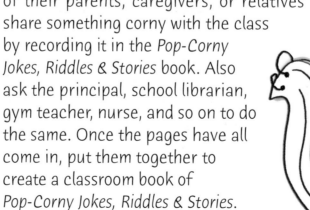

PREDICTIONS SHEET

Names: _____

Predictions:

We predict that _____ tablespoons of kernels will make _____ cups of popped popcorn.

We predict that the first pop will happen ____ minutes ____ seconds after the popcorn popper is turned on.

We predict that the last kernel will pop in ____ minutes ____ seconds.

We predict that there will be _____ kernels that did not pop.

        *   *   *   *   *   *   *   *   *   *   *

Results:

_____ Our prediction was very close to the actual amount of popped popcorn.

_____ Our prediction was too low.

_____ Our prediction was too high.

_____ Our prediction was close to the time it actually took to pop the popcorn.

_____ Our prediction was too low.

_____ Our prediction was too high.

_____ Our prediction was close to the actual number of kernels that did not pop.

_____ Our prediction was too low.

_____ Our prediction was too high.

POP-CORNY BOOK

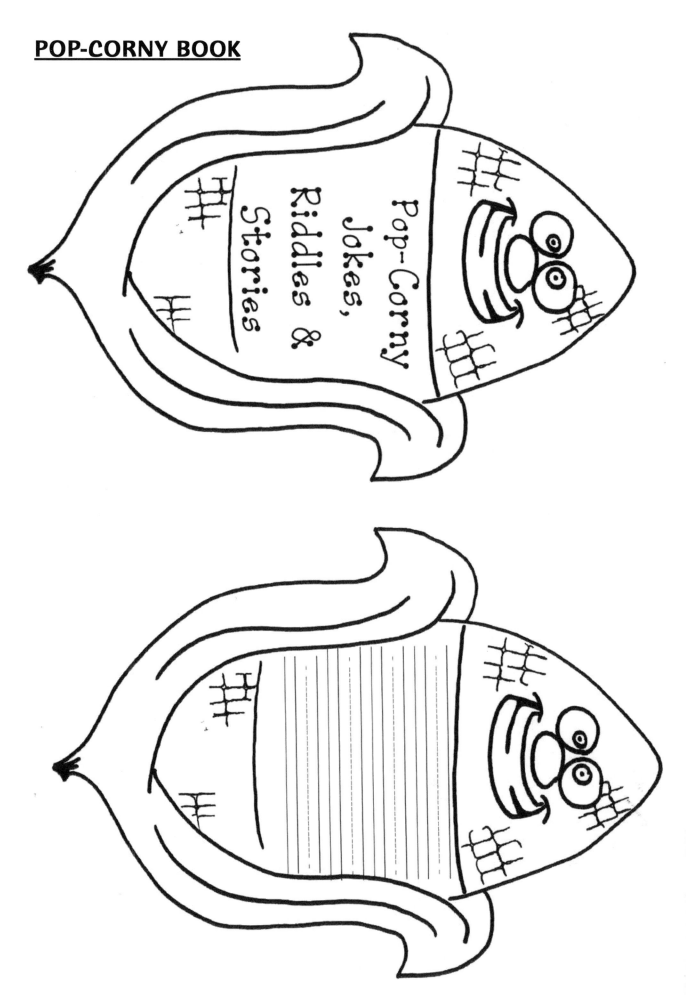

Pop-Corny
Jokes,
Riddles &
Stories

7. Yes, I Love to Move

Tune: "I've Been Working on the Railroad"

I am walking in a circle. I can walk all day.
I am walking in a circle. It's fun to walk this way.

Walking up and down the hallway, careful up and down the stairs.
Only running when I'm outside, walking here and there.

Yes, I love to walk. Yes, I love to walk. Yes, I love to walk all day.
Yes, I love to walk. Yes, I love to walk. Yes, I love to walk all day.

I am swimming with the dolphins, in the deep blue sea.
There with all the other fishes, in the water I will be.

Fins are flying past the shoreline. How I love to ride
The waves that crash along the beaches, swimming with the tide.

Yes, I love to swim. Yes, I love to swim. Yes, I love to swim all day.
Yes, I love to swim. Yes, I love to swim. Yes, I love to swim all day.

I am hopping like a rabbit, down the forest trail.
Jumping up and down the hillside. Try and catch my furry tail.

Ducks may waddle in the water. Monkeys swing through the trees.
But I'm so glad to be a bunny, hopping as I please.

Yes, I love to hop. Yes, I love to hop. Yes, I love to hop all day.
Yes, I love to hop. Yes, I love to hop. Yes, I love to hop all day.

I am crawling like a spider, crawling all around.
I am crawling like a spider, with my eight legs on the ground.

Spinning webs and eating insects. Try to run away.
Crawling up and down your shoulder, spiders love to play.

Yes, I love to crawl. Yes, I love to crawl. Yes, I love to crawl all day.
Yes, I love to crawl. Yes, I love to crawl. Yes, I love to crawl all day.

I am flying like an eagle, soaring way up high.
I am flying like an eagle, gliding in the sky.

Feathers float above the mountain, eyes sharper than a nail.
Diving down to catch my supper, guided by my tail.

Yes, I love to fly. Yes, I love to fly. Yes, I love to fly all day.
Yes, I love to fly. Yes, I love to fly. Yes, I love to fly all day.

MATERIALS:

- visors (available at dollar stores) or painter's caps, 1 for each child
- hat patterns (see pages 61-63)
- construction paper of various colors
- oak tag or poster paper
- wiggly eyes
- Tacky Glue (works best)
- *Dinosaurs, Popcorn, Penguins & More* CD

Give each child a visor or cap and a hat pattern. Ask the children to color their pattern pieces, cut them out, and glue them to their visors or caps (see illustration). The children with the "human" hats can decorate them with smiley faces or however they wish. Put on the "Yes, I Love to Move" song and have the kids wear their hats as they sing and move to the music.

HAT PATTERNS

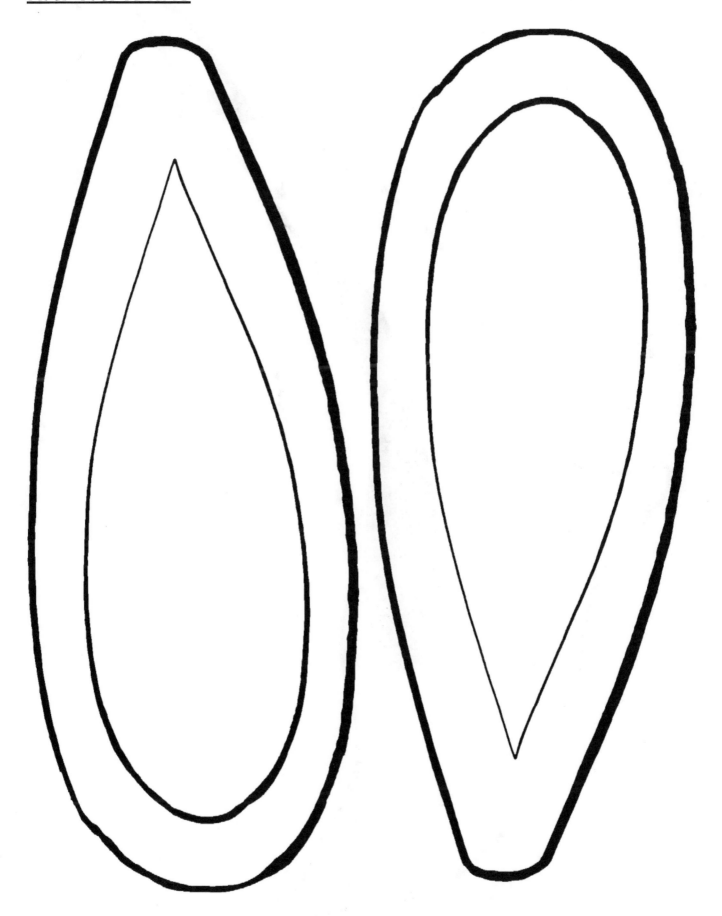

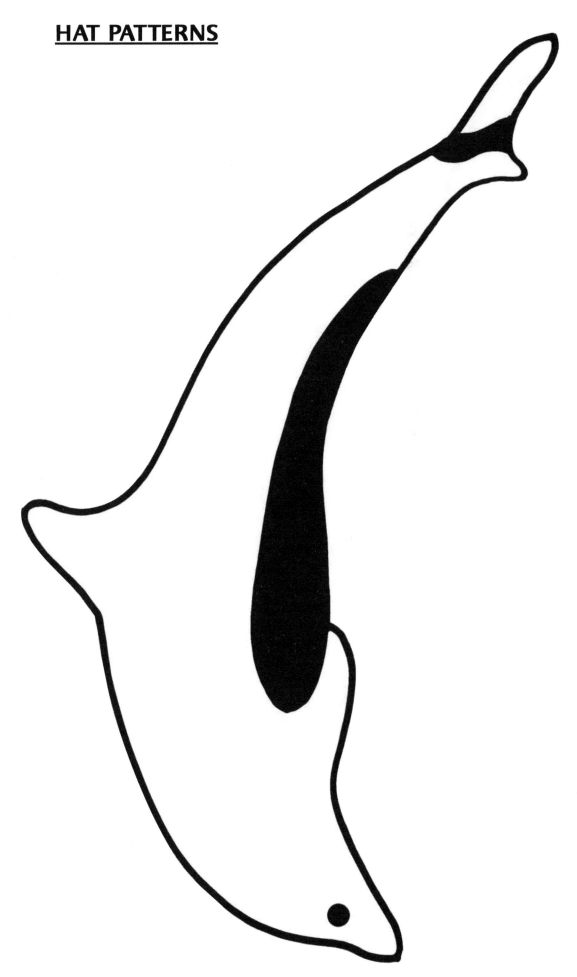

HAT PATTERNS

Smartie Train

MATERIALS:

• train whistle (available from Crystal Springs Books)

Have the children line up like a train. Ask the first child to be the engine and the last child the caboose. Tell the engine to call out a way to get around (such as walk, skip, jump, and so on) and have the other children take turns demonstrating the movement. When everyone in line has done it, blow the whistle, have the engine go to the end of the train, and start the game again.

How People and Animals Get Around

MATERIALS:

Make a list of ways in which people and animals get around (crawl, fly, gallop, walk, pedal, slither, jump, hop, and so on). Choose three ways, write each one at the top of a column, and ask the children to draw or write as many animals or things as they can think of that get around that way. For example:

HOP	FLY	FLOAT
rabbits	birds	lily pads
frogs	bugs	water bugs
grasshoppers	airplanes	boats

Animal Tracks

Show the class a variety of animal tracks, such as those made by a turkey, a rabbit, a coyote, and so on. Let the children select the materials they prefer to create their own sets of tracks, using different colors and shapes.

MATERIALS:

- sponges
- foam pieces
- cotton balls
- macaroni
- ink pads
- paint

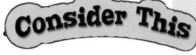

Consider This

Use this as a creative writing activity: have the children describe the animals (or things) that could have created their track prints.

Motion Invention

Brainstorm ways in which people get around. Ask the children to imagine that they are inventors working on new ways to travel from place to place. Explain that sometimes the best part of one invention is added to the best part of another to make a completely new and different invention. One example might be a truck with buggy wheels. Tell the children to use shapes and lines to create new ways to get around.

MATERIALS:

- 14"x18" white drawing paper
- rulers
- rectangular shapes to trace (pencil box, paper clip box, small book, etc.)
- round shapes to trace (spool of thread, can, film container, quarter, etc.)

8. Little Piggies

Tune: "She'll Be Comin' 'Round the Mountain"

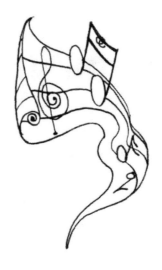

Little piggies rock-and-rollin' in the mud,
Little piggies rock-and-rollin' in the mud,
Rock-and-rollin' little piggies,
Rock-and-rollin' little piggies,
Little piggies rock-and-rollin' in the mud.

Dancin' piggies doin' jiggies in the dirt,
Dancin' piggies doin' jiggies in the dirt,
Oh, those jiggy little piggies,
Little piggies dancin' jiggies,
Dancin' piggies doin' jiggies in the dirt.

Baby piggies have a squiggly, wiggly tail.
Baby piggies have a squiggly, wiggly tail.
Squiggly tails they like to wiggle.
Wiggly tails, they make me giggle.
Baby piggies have a squiggly, wiggly tail.

Squiggly piggies like their bellies tickled too.
Squiggly piggies like their bellies tickled too.
Do you like your belly tickled?
Tickled bellies make me giggle.
Squiggly piggies like their bellies tickled too.

Rub the belly of a piggy that you love.
Rub the belly of a piggy that you love.
Piggy bellies need a rubbin'.
Piggy bellies need some lovin'.
Rub the belly of a piggy that you love.

Singin' piggies oinking oinky-doinky songs,
Singin' piggies oinking oinky-doinky songs,
Oinky-doinky little piggies,
Oinkin' songs and dancin' jiggies,
Singin' piggies oinkin' oinky-doinky songs.

Little piggies rock-and-rollin' in the dirt,
Dancin' piggies doing jiggies in the dirt,
Oh, those jiggy little piggies,
Dancin', singin' little jiggies,
Giggly, wiggly little piggies in the dirt.

Little piggies rock-and-rollin' in the mud,
Little piggies rock-and-rollin' in the mud,
Rock-and-rollin' little piggies,
Rock-and-rollin' little piggies,
Little piggies rock-and-rollin' in the mud.

Piggy Polka

Tell the children to decorate, cut out, and assemble their Piggy Masks. Play the "Little Piggies" song. Tell the children to put on their masks and create a pig dance to go along with the music by oinking, wiggling their tails, and moving to the beat.

MATERIALS:

- pink masks (available at party stores), 1 for each child
- pink foam (for nose and ears)
- *Dinosaurs, Popcorn, Penguins & More* CD

Milk Cap Piggy Pin

Model how to make the piggy pin and then give the children materials so that they can make their own. Glue the wiggly eyes and a pink pony bead for the nose on the front of the milk cap. Add a small piece of yarn for the mouth. Attach two pieces of pink foam for the ears, and glue the pin clasp onto the back (inside) of the cap.

front

back

MATERIALS:

- milk caps
- wiggly eyes
- pink pony beads
- pin clasps
- yarn (mouths)
- pink foam (ears)

Mini Piggy Bank

MATERIALS:

- black film containers with lids, 1 for each child
- black pony beads
- pink pony beads
- pipe cleaners
- wiggly eyes
- black construction paper (piggy mouths)
- pink construction paper (piggy ears)

Cut a vertical opening into the side of each film container, making sure it's large enough for coins to fit through. Give the children their own containers and then model how to make the piggy bank so that they can create their own. On the side directly opposite the vertical opening, glue four black pony beads for the piggy's legs (see illustration). Wrap a 1-to-2-inch piece of pipe cleaner around a pencil to make a curly tail. Pierce a hole in the bottom of the film container, push one end of the curled pipe cleaner into the hole, and bend the end inside the container to hold it in place. On the container lid, glue two eyes, a pink pony bead for the nose, two pink ears, and a small black mouth. Put the lid on the container, and the piggy bank is ready to use.

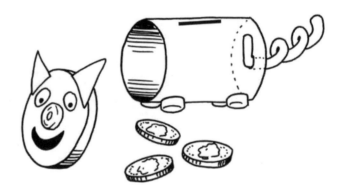

This is an enjoyable gift-making project for children.

Tongue Twisters

Referring to the illustration, punch two holes in a manila folder. Line up multiple copies of the Tongue Twister sheet and punch holes in the tops of those pages. Hold them in place with brass fasteners. Tape or glue the white envelope onto the opposite side of the folder so that you can open the flap side. Make up a tongue twister and use the black marker to write it on the sentence strip. Start with something simple, such as "Bob blows bubbles." Underline the first word with green marker and the punctuation at the end with red marker. Cut the sentence into words and place the words in the envelope. Give the folder to a child and ask her to use the visual clues to figure out how the sentence strip goes together. (Clues: Green underline stands for "go," meaning the first word in the sentence. Red underline stands for "stop," meaning the punctuation at the end of the sentence.) Once she figures out the order, have her copy the sentence onto the Tongue Twister sheet and illustrate it. Keep multiple copies of the Tongue Twister sheet in the folder so that when one child finishes, she can pull out her sheet and leave the folder for others to use.

MATERIALS:
- manila file folders
- white business envelopes
- sentence strips
- red, black, and green markers
- "Tongue Twister" sheets (see page 70)
- hole punch
- brass fasteners

Consider This

To make it easier for children to sequence the words, cut them apart into puzzle-shaped pieces.

TONGUE TWISTER

Name

Illustrate the tongue twister

Pigsty

Make multiple copies of the piggy on pink paper, cut them out, and tape them to index cards. Use the remaining index cards for the letters, words, or concepts you want to teach. Laminate the cards to make them more durable. Have the children sit in a circle. Place the cards face side down in the center and spread the cards out in a circle. Ask each child to take a turn picking one card from the circle. One by one, have each child look at his card and read what it says. If he is correct, he keeps the card. If incorrect, he turns the card face side up and the teacher says the letter, word, or concept, and then returns the card to the center. The next child may choose that card and say the correct answer, or select any other card and read what it says. The game continues around the circle. When a child picks up one of the piggy cards, everyone in the circle jumps up, turns around, and yells, "Oink! Oink! Oink!" When the teacher calls, "Pigsty!" everyone sits back down, the teacher gets the piggy card, and the game continues. The game ends when all the cards have been identified.

MATERIALS

- "Piggy" reproducible (below)

- pink construction paper

- index cards

- letters, words, or concepts (such as the alphabet, sight words, color words, student names, etc.)

To increase attention skills (kids love to *oink*), place several piggy cards in with the concept cards. As children pay more attention to the game, start weeding out the piggy cards so that you spend more time on the concepts.

"Piggy" reproducible

9. Penguins

Tune: "Oh! Susanna"

A penguin walking down the street waddled up to me.
His coat was black. His shirt was white, had a yellow pointed beak.
Penguins breathe air and lay eggs, like their feathered friends,
But if they really want to fly, they'll just have to pretend.

CHORUS
Mr. Penguin, I can't teach you to fly.
Like the birds and the bees and the bugs that soar,
Way up in the sky.

He likes the cold and loves the snow and swims Antarctic seas.
He lives with other penguins in a penguin colony.
His wings are more like flippers and his feathers keep him dry,
Fishing in the ocean, swimming with the tide.

CHORUS

Hopping into town that day, he saw an eagle soar.
He tried and tried so hard to fly, but his feet stayed on the floor.
He asked me if I'd help him learn to fly like other birds.
Can a talking penguin learn to fly? I think that sounds absurd.

CHORUS repeats 2 times

Penguin Comparison

Draw a Venn diagram on large chart paper or the blackboard. Tell the children to compare penguins with other birds, describing how they are alike and how they are different. Fill in the Venn diagram with the information they tell you. Give each child an opportunity to choose a specific bird with which to compare the penguin. (Don't forget the ostrich, another bird that does not fly.)

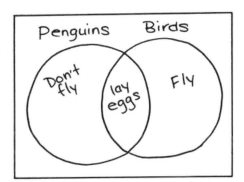

Penguin Parade

Trace the patterns onto the colored paper; make a set for each child. Model how to assemble the hat and then have the children cut out their pattern pieces and glue or tape them together. (The oak tag or poster paper makes the hat sturdier; it will stay on the child's head more easily.) Ask each child to write her name on the inside of her hat (the oak tag part) so you can quickly pass them out each time you use them. Play the song and have the children wear their hats while singing and parading around the room.

MATERIALS:
- large chart paper

MATERIALS:
- "Penguin Hat" patterns (see page 74)
- black, white, and yellow construction paper
- oak tag or poster paper
- giant wiggly eyes (optional)
- *Dinosaur, Popcorn, Penguins & More* CD

1

2

3

A

B

C

Instructions for the Penguin Hat

1. Make enlarged photocopy of pattern piece A. Trace and cut from 11"x17" piece of black construction paper.

2. Trace and cut two eyes (pattern piece B) from white paper. Glue on wiggly eyes and then attach to black head shape.

3. Trace and cut beak (pattern piece C) from piece of yellow construction paper and glue to front of black head shape.

4. Trace and cut pattern piece A from 8 ½"x11" piece of oak tag. Overlap flaps 1, 2, and 3, adjusting to fit child's head, and staple together.

5. Overlap flaps on black head shape and staple together.

6. Place oak tag shape inside black head shape and staple together at back. Glue or tape front of oak tag shape to inside of black head shape.

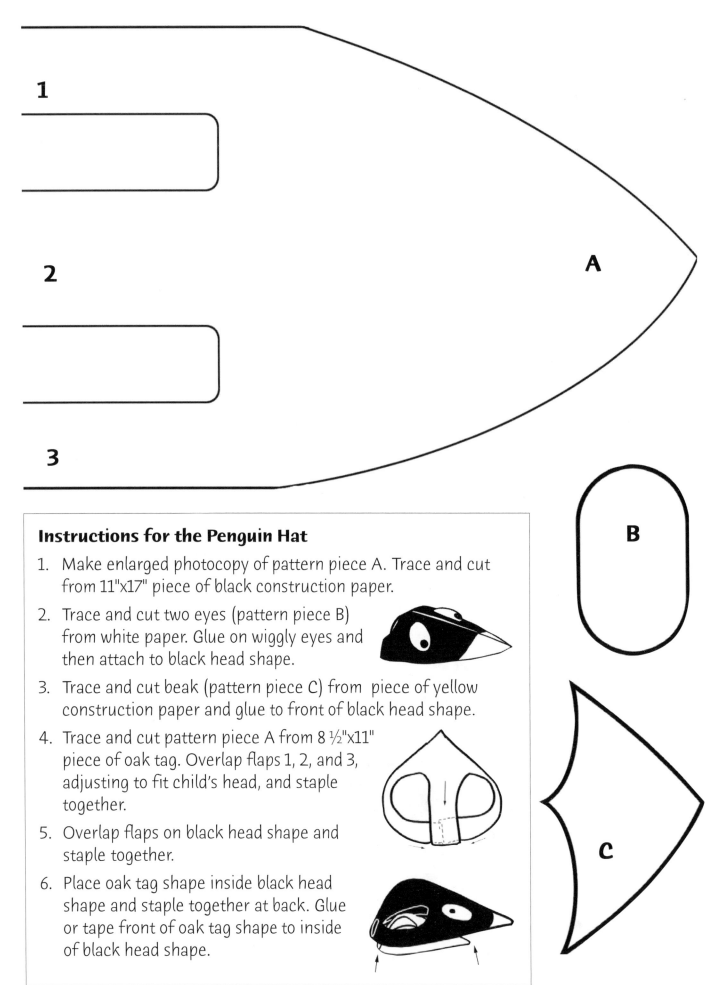

Did You Know ...? Book

Tell the children to stack their sheets of paper together, fold them in half crosswise (hamburger style) and then in half again. Have them staple the sheets in three or four places along the folded side on the left and close to the edge. Tell them to cut along the folded edges on the tops of the pages, creating a book with eight pages, front and back. Play the song again and ask the children to write in their books the things they learned about penguins and to include a drawing for each. For example, penguins are black and white with a yellow beak, breathe air, lay eggs, don't fly, like cold and love snow, live in colonies, swim in the ocean, have wings like flippers, have feathers to keep them dry. (You might want to list these on the blackboard as the song plays so that the children can refer to them while writing.) Before they start drawing, show them how to dip a thumb into the ink pad, press it on a page in the book, and turn it into a "Penguin Print."

MATERIALS:
- 8½"x11" sheets of paper, 2 for each child
- washable black ink pad
- *Dinosaurs, Popcorn, Penguins & More* CD

Penguin Diorama

Fold one square of white paper in half diagonally and then in half once again (see step 1.). Open the paper and cut along one of the fold lines to the center of the paper, creating two flaps (see step 2.). Slide one flap over the other to form a triangular, self-standing background (see step 3.). Staple, glue, or tape it to hold it in position. Repeat with the other square, and then staple the two pieces together to form a double diorama (see steps 4. and 5.).

Give each child a copy of the reproducible and have him color and cut out two penguin scenes of his choice. Before the children attach the penguins to their dioramas, ask them to create backgrounds for both, such as the ocean for the swimming penguin and a nest for the adult and egg or adult and baby penguin (see step 6.). After all the children have finished their dioramas, display them together as a "Penguin Colony."

MATERIALS:

- 2 squares (8½"x8½") of plain white paper for each child
- "Penguins" reproducible (see page 77)

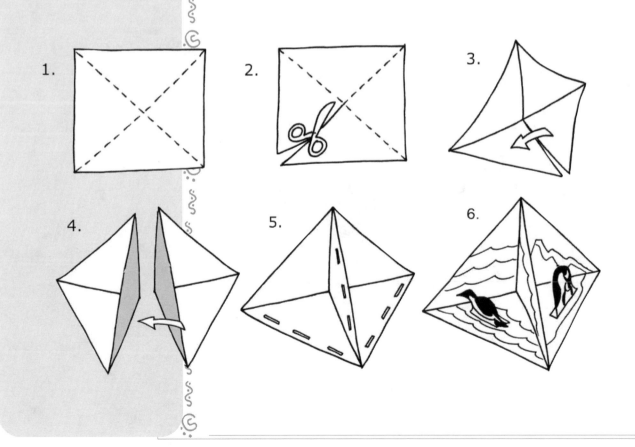

PENGUINS

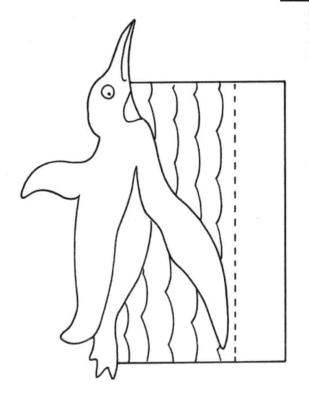

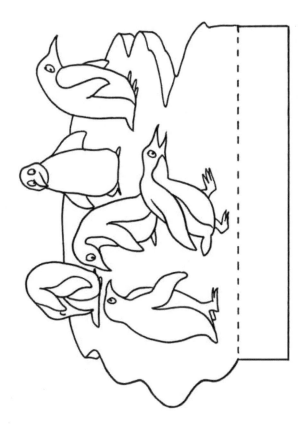

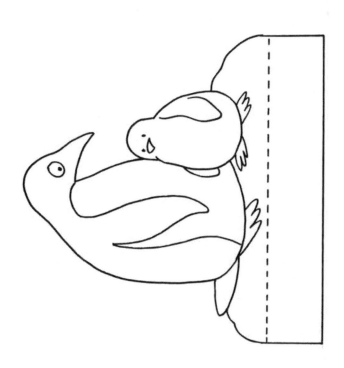

10. Where Do I Live?

Tune: "My Bonnie Lies Over the Ocean"

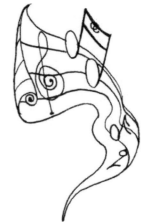

I live in a home with my family.
It's here that I sleep, eat, and play.
I read in my bed with my teddy.
We're learning new things every day.

I live, I live, I live with my family.
I live, I live, I live with my family.

Swimming way out in the ocean,
My fins help me glide through the sea.
My gills are for breathing in water.
There's no place that I'd rather be.
I live in a shell by the water.
It's small but it's cozy to me.
My claws and my body fit nicely.
My shell is my home by the sea.

I live, I live, the sea is where you'll find me.
I live, I live, the sea is where you'll find me.

I live in a tree in the jungle,
Swinging on branches and vines,
Peeling and eating bananas,
Having fun all of the time.
I live in a nest with my mother.
She brings me worms every day.
My feathers and wings they keep growing,
And someday I'll fly away.

I live, I live, I live up in a tree.
I live, I live, I live up in a tree.

I live in a hole called a burrow,
Under the ground by a tree.
I hop through the forest each morning.
My big ears flop free in the breeze.
I live in a cave in the forest.
In the winter it's where I will stay.
I sleep when it's snowy and cold out,
And wait for a much warmer day.

I live, I live, the forest is where I will be.
I live, I live, the forest is where I will be.

New Verse

Have the children sing along as you play the song "Where Do I Live?" Then ask them to fill out their New Verse sheets with their own lyrics about something that lives somewhere. When they have finished writing, tell them to illustrate their pages and then sing their songs to the class if they'd like.

Who Lives Here? Book

Make an eight-page book for each child from the Who Lives Here? reproducible and staple the pages together along the left side. Have the children color their book pages and the Where Do I Live? reproducible, and then cut out the animals. While playing the song, have the children follow along in their books and decide where each animal belongs. Then have them glue the animals to the correct pages.

Who lives here?

NEW VERSE FOR "WHERE DO I LIVE?"

I live _____

It's here that I

_____

I live, I live,

_____

I live, I live,

_____

NEW VERSE FOR "WHERE DO I LIVE?"

I live _____

It's here that I

_____

I live, I live,

_____

I live, I live,

_____

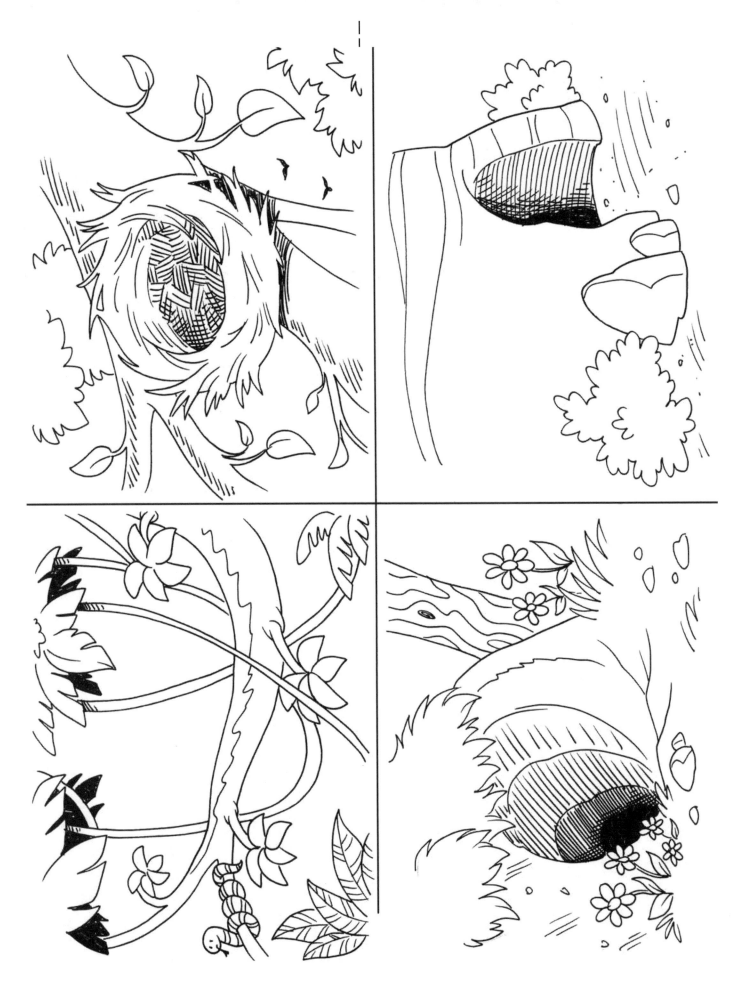

WHERE DO I LIVE?

Guess Who? Riddle Book

MATERIALS:

- construction paper
- "Door" reproducible (see page 85)
- "Clues" sheet (see page 85)

Give each child the Door reproducible and Clues sheet. Tell each child to decorate the door and then cut along the lines on the top and bottom of the door. Have each child glue the frame of the door to her construction paper (see illustration), and be sure to point out that she shouldn't glue the door itself. Have each child "open" the door and draw a picture of a person or glue a picture of someone from a magazine, without telling anyone who the person is. The picture may be of a classmate, someone who works at your school, a famous author or sports figure, and so on. Have each child write on the Clues sheet three clues about who is hiding behind the door, and paste the sheet on the other side of the construction paper, across from the door. When everyone has finished, put all together to create a classroom riddle book.

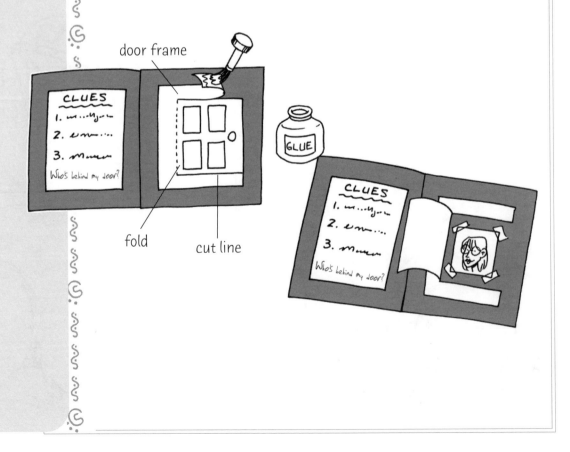

door frame

fold

cut line

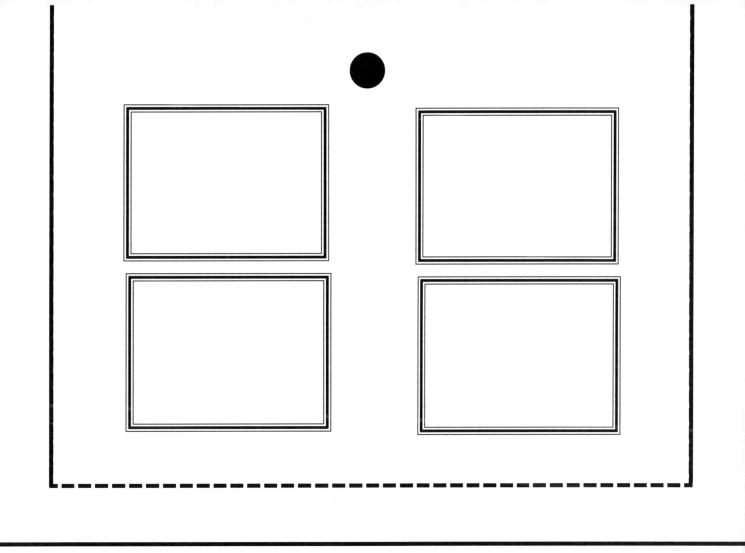

CLUES

1.

2.

3.

Who's behind my door?

Animal Research

MATERIALS:

- "Animal Research Guide" (see page 87)

During this independent research activity, brainstorm with the whole class or with each individual child about the animal(s) of interest. Tell the children that they can do their research in a variety of ways: for example, on the Internet, by reading books and magazines, or by talking with a veterinarian or a person who has the same kind of animal. Give them each a copy of the Animal Research Guide to fill out and return to you when it's completed.

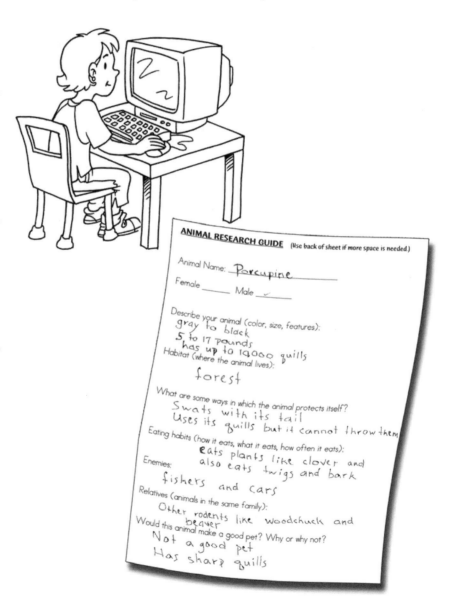

ANIMAL RESEARCH GUIDE (Use back of sheet if more space is needed.)

Animal Name: Porcupine

Female _____ Male ✓

Describe your animal (color, size, features):
gray to black
5 to 17 pounds
has up to 10000 quills
Habitat (where the animal lives):

forest

What are some ways in which the animal protects itself?
Swats with its tail
Uses its quills but it cannot throw them
Eating habits (how it eats, what it eats, how often it eats):
eats plants like clover and
also eats twigs and bark
Enemies:
fishers and cars
Relatives (animals in the same family):
Other rodents like woodchuck and
beaver
Would this animal make a good pet? Why or why not?
Not a good pet
Has sharp quills

ANIMAL RESEARCH GUIDE (Use back of sheet if more space is needed.)

Animal Name: _____

Female _____ Male _____

Describe your animal (color, size, features):

Habitat (where the animal lives):

What are some ways in which the animal protects itself?

Eating habits (how it eats, what it eats, how often it eats):

Enemies:

Relatives (animals in the same family):

Would this animal make a good pet? Why or why not?

11. I Know I Know So Many Things

Tune: "The Muffin Man"

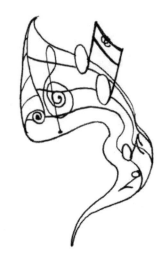

CHORUS:

I know I know so many things,
So many things, so many things.
I know I know so many things,
So many things I know.

Can you shout your name out loud?
Your name out loud? Your name out loud?
Can you shout your name out loud?
Shout it loud and clear!

Do you know your birthday date?
Your birthday date? Your birthday date?
Do you know your birthday date?
The date that you were born.

Do you know what time it is?
What time it is? What time it is?
Do you know what time it is?
The hands, they tell the time.

Do you know your teacher's name?
Your teacher's name? Your teacher's name?
Do you know your teacher's name?
Your teacher's name is _____!

Do you know where you live?
Where you live? Where you live?
Do you know where you live?
The number, street, and town.

Do you know your phone number?
Your phone number? Your phone number?
Do you know your phone number?
I'll call you on the phone.

Do you know the quiet sign?
The quiet sign? The quiet sign?
Do you know the quiet sign?
The sign to quiet down.

CHORUS repeats 2 times

Things I Know Book

Tell the children to fold their sheets of paper in half crosswise (hamburger style), creating four-page books. Tell each child to write his name and the title *I Know So Many Things* on the first page. Have the children write or draw on the following pages some of the things they can do. They can choose from the List of Possibilities sheet and/or come up with other things they know how to do.

List of Possibilities

I know:

My name	My address
My mom's and dad's names	My phone number
My ABCs	My manners
How to draw	How to write
How to read	How to retell a story
How to share	How to be a leader
How to tie my shoes	How to add
How to count to _____	How to subtract
How to sharpen my pencil	_____ Popcorn Words
How to open my milk carton	

Things We Know Chart

MATERIALS:

- chart paper
  or whiteboard

This is an ongoing activity to do over time with your children. Create a chart that lists things the children may know (see illustration). From time to time, ask the children how many of them know how to do the things on the chart. Go down the list, have them raise their hands if they know how, count the hands, and write the number on the chart. Some weeks later, ask again, count the hands, and change the number (which, hopefully, is increasing!). Highlight the number when all the children know. This chart is a great visual to share with parents to show what the class has learned.

Do You Know Me?

MATERIALS:

- reproducible
  sheets
  (see page 91)

This is a fun activity for Open House. Give a copy of the reproducible sheet, folded in half lengthwise (hot-dog style), to each child's parents and have them fill out one side. Have the child fill out the other side and then look at his parents' answers and give them a grade based on what they wrote.

I /We Know
_____'s

FAVORITES

Food _____

Lunch_____

Color_____

Book_____

Person_____

Animal _____

Things about school _____

Things to do_____

I love_____

I don't like_____

Message_____

I /We Know

_____'s

FAVORITES

Food _____

Lunch_____

Color_____

Book_____

Person_____

Animal_____

Things about school

_____

Things to do

_____

I love

_____

I don't like

_____

Message

_____

_____

_____

Name _____

MY FAVORITES

Food _____

Lunch_____

Color_____

Book_____

Person_____

Animal_____

Things about school

_____

Things to do

_____

I love

_____

I don't like

_____

Message

_____

_____

"Me" Mobile

MATERIALS:

- "Mobile" reproducible (see page 93)
- hole punch
- ribbon or strings of different lengths

Make enlarged copies of the reproducible on colored paper or have the children color and cut out the pieces. Tell them to write the following information:

- On the header, write your name.
- On the brain, draw or write 3 things you know.
- On the hands, draw or write 2 things your hands can do.
- On the treasure box, draw or write some of your favorite things.
- On the crystal ball, draw or write what you see in your future.

Tell the children to punch a hole in each piece and then tie a different length of ribbon or string to each piece. Have them punch four holes in the header and attach the mobile pieces to it. To hang the mobile, punch another hole in the top of the header, attach ribbon or string, and suspend where there will be room for the pieces to move.

To level the activity, leave out the number of things the children should write on the mobile pieces.

Parent/Friend Survey

MATERIALS:

- "Survey" sheet (see page 95)

Tell each student to talk with another child or with an adult about the questions on his survey sheet, to find out something unusual that the person can do. After the kids fill out their sheets and/or draw pictures based on the information they were told, have them return the surveys to you to share with the class.

I Know My Teacher

MATERIALS:

- "I Know My Teacher" sheet (see page 96)

After a few months together in class, it is amazing to see how much children do and do not know about you. Ask them to fill out copies of the sheet to the best of their knowledge and to guess when they aren't sure. Answers are heartwarming, funny, and enlightening!

<u>SURVEY</u>

Student's Name _____

Participant's Name _____

Questions for student to ask:
What unusual or interesting thing can you do?

_____

_____

When did you learn or discover this?

_____

_____

If you learned it, who or what taught you?

_____

    *   *   *   *   *   *   *   *   *   *

How would you (the student) describe this?
Silly _____ Funny _____ Unusual _____ Interesting _____ Cool _____
One in a Million _____ Scary _____ Amazing _____
Or _____

Draw it!

I KNOW MY TEACHER

My teacher's first name is _____

Birthday month _____ Where born? _____

Married? _____ Husband's/wife's name _____

Kids? _____ How many? _____ Kid's name(s) _____

Kind of car _____ Color _____

Favorite color _____

Favorite food _____

Favorite book _____

Favorite animal _____

Favorite TV show _____

What time does your teacher:

Come to school _____ Leave school _____

What are your teacher's hobbies?_____

_____

What is your teacher's favorite thing to say?

" _____ "

_____

12. I Brush My Teeth So Clean

Tune: "When Johnny Comes Marching Home"

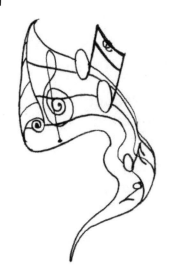

I brush my teeth three times a day. So clean! So clean!
I brush and floss the germs away. So clean! So clean!
My smile is wide. My teeth are white.
Morning, noon, and every night.
My mouth is clean, clean, clean. So clean. So clean. So clean.

I never want a cavity. So clean! So clean!
My teeth, they mean so much to me. So clean! So clean!
My dentist says, "There's no decay,"
Because I chase the germs away and
My mouth is clean, clean, clean. So clean. So clean. So clean.

Mouthwash makes my mouth feel clean. So clean! So clean!
I swish it 'round, then down the drain. So clean! So clean!
I gargle with it every day,
It tastes real bad, but that's okay.
My mouth is clean, clean, clean. So clean. So clean. So clean.

I brush my teeth three times a day. So clean! So clean!
I brush and floss the germs away. So clean! So clean!
My smile is wide. My teeth are white.
Morning, noon, and every night.
My mouth is clean, clean, clean. So clean. So clean. So clean.

I always watch the food I eat. So clean! So clean!
I stay away from sugar sweet. So clean! So clean!
It tastes so good, but it's so bad,
It rots my teeth and makes me sad.
My mouth is clean, clean, clean. So clean. So clean. So clean.

A healthy mouth means no decay. So clean! So clean!
Bacteria have gone away. So clean! So clean!
My gums are strong, my teeth are bright,
I clean and brush and floss each night.
My mouth is clean, clean, clean. So clean. So clean. So clean.

I brush my teeth three times a day. So clean! So clean!
I brush and floss the germs away. So clean! So clean!
My smile is wide. My teeth are white.
Morning, noon, and every night.
My mouth is clean, clean, clean. So clean. So clean. So clean.

Tooth Mobile

MATERIALS:

- "Tooth Mobile" reproducible (see page 100)
- sheets of paper, white and various colors
- crêpe paper, yarn, or ribbon of different lengths

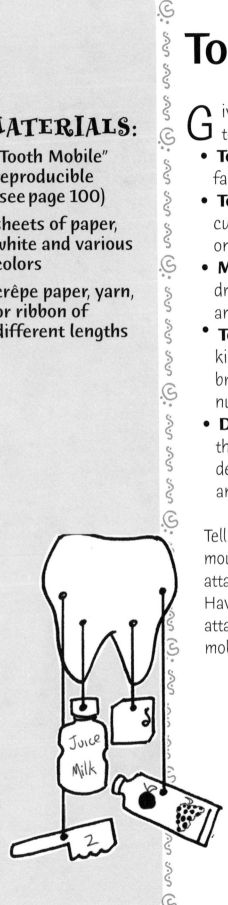

Give the children enlarged copies of the mobile pieces to trace as follows:

- **Tooth on white paper**. Write about or draw the tooth fairy's house on the tooth.
- **Toothpaste tube on paper of any color**. Draw or cut out food ads for three healthy snacks and glue them onto the tube.
- **Mouthwash bottle on paper of any color**. Write or draw three things you like to drink, and say why they are or are not good for you.
- **Toothbrush on paper of any color**. Survey all other kids in the class and tally the number of times they brush their teeth each day. Record the most common number on the paper.
- **Dental floss on paper of any color**. Write or draw three ways to take care of your teeth (for example: see dentist, brush, floss, don't use teeth as a tool, eat right, and so on).

Tell the children to punch a hole in the toothpaste tube, mouthwash bottle, toothbrush, and dental floss, and attach a piece of crêpe paper, yarn, or ribbon to each. Have each child punch four holes in her paper tooth, attach the other pieces to it, and then suspend the mobile.

Dental Care Book

Make six enlarged copies of just the tooth. Cut out a circle the same size and in the same place on the first five teeth, and draw a circle the same size and in the same place on the sixth tooth. Write one of the following sentences on five of the teeth:

> I take care of my teeth.
> I brush my teeth.
> I floss.
> I use mouthwash.
> I see the dentist.

On the sixth tooth draw a line under the circle and write "Name" below it. Make a set of six teeth for each child. Cut a slit in two places on the tooth that reads "I floss." Give each child a picture of herself and a piece of dental floss. Tell each child to glue her photo in the circle on the last tooth (the last page of the book). Have each student also thread the dental floss through the slits on the "I floss" page. Tell each child to stack the six teeth together so that all the holes line up and the picture shows through on the last page. Have the students staple the teeth together in two places along the left side to form a book, and let them take their books home to show their families.

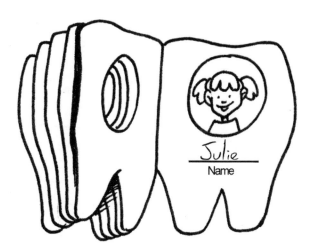

Julie
Name

1 | 2 | 3 | other

Missing Tooth Graph

Tack the Ziploc bags to a bulletin board. Place the numbered cards 0 to 4 above the bags in numerical order. Give the children their name cards and tell them to place their cards in the bag representing the number of front teeth they're missing. For example, if a child is missing two front teeth, she places her name card into the Ziploc bag below the number 2. This information will change over time and can be used for estimation: Which bag has the most cards? What information does that tell us about our class at this point in time?

MATERIALS:

- 5 quart-size Ziploc bags
- cards printed with children's names, 1 per card
- 5 cards, numbered 0 to 4
- tacks

a. It's fun to tape the child's picture to his name card too.

b. To simplify the activity, use only two bags—"Yes" and "No"—and ask the children whether they're missing any front teeth.

13. The People in Our School

Tune: "The Wheels on the Bus"

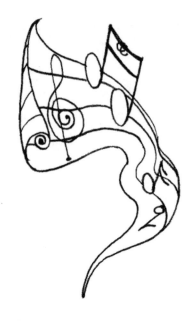

The people in our school say, "Hi there, kids.
Hi there, kids. Hi there, kids."
The people in our school say, "Hi there,
kids."
All through the halls.
The principal says, "Come join our team.
Join our team, join our team."
The principal says, "Come join our team."
All through the halls.
The school nurse says, "How do you feel?
Do you feel? Do you feel?"
The school nurse says, "How do you feel?
How do you feel today?"
My music teacher loves to sing,
Loves to sing, loves to sing.
My music teacher loves to sing.
She helps me sing along.

My gym teacher says, "Let's exercise,
Exercise, exercise."
My gym teacher says, "Let's exercise.
It's good for girls and boys."
The lunch lady says, "It's time for lunch.
Time for lunch, time for lunch."
The lunch lady says, "It's time for lunch.
What would you like today?"
Librarians help us find good books,
Find good books, find good books.
You sign them out and take them home.
Read a book today.
My art teacher says, "Let's all have fun,

All have fun, all have fun."
My art teacher says, "Let's all have fun."
It's fun to paint and draw.
My friends at school all love to learn,
Love to learn, love to learn.
My friends at school all love to learn.
School's the place to be.

Our School Address Book

This is a good activity to use at the beginning of the year. Give all the children a copy of the reproducible. Have them cut it apart, stack the 4 pages together, and then staple them along the left side, creating a 4-page book. Tell them to fill in people's names and their numbers as you call them out or as you write them on the blackboard or overhead. Let them fill in the blank page with the name of a person of their choice—the librarian, art teacher, music teacher, gym teacher, etc. Have the children decorate each page with a drawing of the person or of something that each person does.

MATERIALS:

• "Our School Address Book" reproducible (see page 104)

The school nurse's name is
Mrs. Brown
The phone number is
555-1212 ex 123

The art teachers's name is
Mrs. Fox
The phone number is
555-1212 ex 345

The principal's name is
_____.

The phone number is
_____.

The school nurse's name is
_____.

The phone number is
_____.

The school secretary's name is
_____.

The phone number is
_____.

The _____'s name is
_____.

The phone number is
_____.

Job Description Book

Give each of the children a picture of one person from the reproducible. Ask each child to think of one, two, or three things that the person at school has to do as part of his or her job and to write those duties under the picture. For the principal, for example, kids may say things such as "give out pencils," "wave to the buses," and "talk to kids who don't behave." Sometimes the answers will be things that the kids have observed the person doing but that have nothing to do with the job. For example, a child in one of my classes once said that our principal's job was to "eat carrots," because he often witnessed Mr. Fencer munching on carrots. Responses are often cute and funny. Collect all the sheets, bind together as desired, and share with others at school. This can be a great introduction to talking about what the people at your school actually do.

MATERIALS:

- sheets of paper
- stapler, binding rib, or chicken ring (rings available from Crystal Springs Books)
- "People in Our School" cards (see page 106)

Our principal gives out pencils.

a. Instead of the reproducible, give kids actual photographs of people in their school.

b. These books make nice gifts for the people about whom the kids are writing and are sure to make them smile.

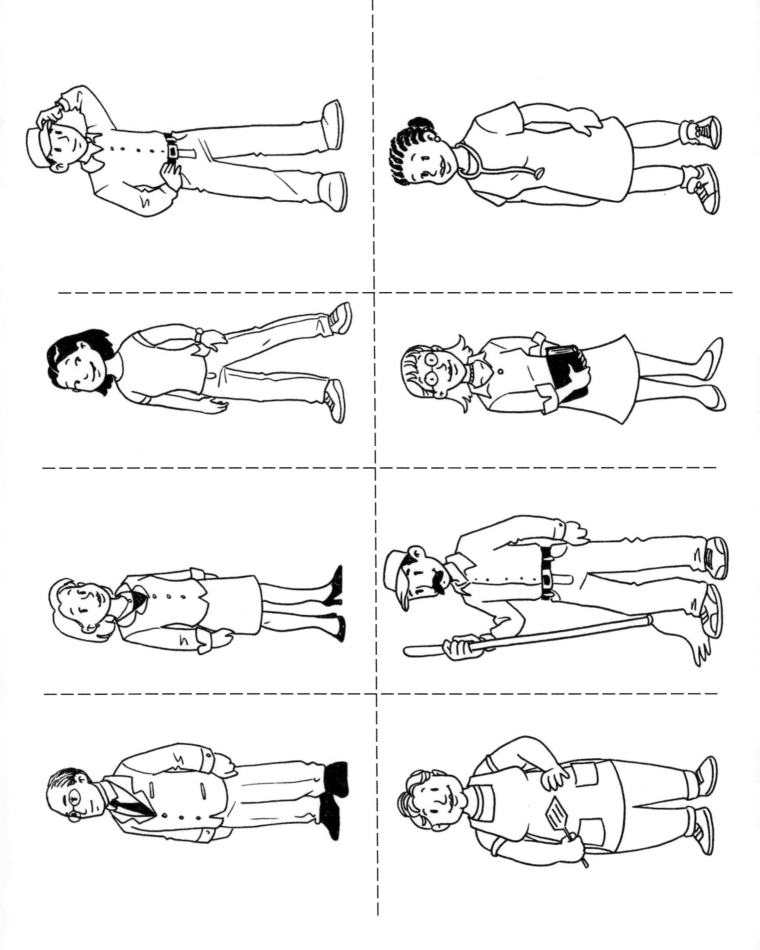

Memory Bags

Provide Associative Memory cards to help children remember people or items in their school, or a particular subject or place that the children have studied. For example, a bookmark might remind a child of the library, the librarian, or the librarian's name: bookmark = library = Mrs. Black. Using the cards reproducible and/or creating others of your own, ask the children to recall what each means and how it helps them remember. Store the cards in Ziploc bags.

MATERIALS:
• "Associative Memory" cards (see page 108)
• Ziploc bags

Consider This

When possible, use the actual item itself instead of the card, such as a real Band-Aid, plastic spoon, napkin, and so forth.

Interactive Songbook

MATERIALS:

- 8½"x11" sheets of paper
- *Dinosaurs, Popcorn, Penguins & More* CD

Give each child a 10-page book that consists of five 8½"x11" sheets of paper, folded in half crosswise (hamburger style), and stapled along the fold. The first page is the cover and has the title of the song "The People in Our School" printed on it; the second page has words from the first verse ("Hi there, kids. Hi there, kids. Hi there, kids.") and a simple line drawing of people in school; the third page has words from the next verse ("Come join our team. Join our team, join our team.") and a picture of the principal; and so forth. Tell the kids to color the drawings in their books. When they have finished, play the song on the CD and have them sing along and follow along in their books as they "read" the words.

Make enlarged copies of the song and let the children cut out the appropriate lines and tape or glue them in their books.

I Have ... Who Has?

MATERIALS:

• "I have ....
Who has...?"
reproducible
(see page 111)

This game can be played with any number of cards as long as you have only one Start Card and one End Card. Each child can play with one or multiple cards. Fill in the cards as you like, photocopy the number you need based on your class size, and pass them out. Begin the game by asking, "Who has the Start Card?" The child with that card stands up and reads his card, "I have the Start Card," and then he reads: "Who has ...?" The child with that card stands up and says, "I have ... . Who has ...?" and so forth. The kids can sit or stand, and then get in line when their cards come up.

☺ *Start*	I have	I have
Who has	Who has	Who has
I have	I have	I have
Who has	Who has	Who has
I have	I have	I have
Who has	Who has	*The End!* ☺

People in Our School Questionnaire

MATERIALS:

- "Important Person" letter (see below)
- "Important Person Questionnaire" (see page 113)

Kids love to know about the people at school. Ask each child to sign his name to the letter, and send it along with the questionnaire to a person in your school. Ask that person to fill out the questionnaire and then return it to you to share with the class. This activity can help make these people more "real" for kids. Some neat people to contact include the principal, the school secretary, aides, the bus driver, cafeteria employees, and custodians.

Dear Important Person,

Our class is gathering information about the people who work in our school. We would love to know about you! Please take a few minutes to share with us any or all of the information on the questionnaire. You are important to us here at school, and we would really like to know more about you.

Thanks for your help!

_____   _____
Teacher's Name   Grade

_____   _____
Student's Name   Student's Name

_____   _____
Student's Name   Student's Name

_____   _____
Student's Name   Student's Name

_____   _____
Student's Name   Student's Name

_____   _____
Student's Name   Student's Name

IMPORTANT PERSON QUESTIONNAIRE

What is your name? _____

What is your job at school? _____

What is the best thing about your job? _____

What do you like least about your job? _____

Personal Information:

What is your favorite food? _____

What is your favorite TV show? _____

What is your favorite book? _____

Check the things that you like to read:

Magazines _____ Newspaper _____ Books _____ Other: _____

Do you have any pets? _____ What kind? _____

How many brothers _____ and sisters _____ do you have?

Name a person whom you "look up to": _____

What do you like to do when you are not at school? _____

_____

Children's Questions:

_____

_____

_____

14. Trash in the Can

Tune: "Home, Home on the Range"

Oh, give me a broom
And a dirty old room,
And I'll clean till my fingers are sore.
I'll sweep up the dirt,
I don't care if it hurts,
'Cause I don't want that grime on my floor.

CHORUS:
Trash, trash in the can,
You can help by lending a hand.
Throw garbage away, tidy up every day,
And the Earth will be happy again.

The rivers and streams
Used to be very clean,
And the turtles and fish loved to play.
But pollution turned bad
All the good times they had,
Now they're crying most every day.

CHORUS

All over the land,
We will do what we can,
We will fight for the right to be clean.
So pitch in, my friend,
We will fight till the end,
The environment wants to be green.

Help every way,
And recycle each day,
Sorting plastic, paper, and cans.
This helps to cut down
What ends up in the ground,
Taking care of our place on this land.

CHORUS repeats 2 times

How Can We Help?

Ask each child to trace both hands on a sheet of paper, then cut out both hands and the world. Have each child glue or tape the world on another sheet of paper and then attach the hands so it looks as though the child's hands are holding the world. Brainstorm with the children the things that we all can do to help make the world a better place. Have the children write or draw some of these things in different places on their papers.

MATERIALS:

- sheets of paper
- "World" reproducible (see page 116)

Graph the Trash

Have each child take a copy of the Recycling Record home and keep track of the number of recyclables there that the family throws away over a specific number of days. How many cans? How many bundles of newspapers? How many plastic jugs or containers? Transfer the collected information onto a large classroom graph showing what all the children's homes threw away over the same time period. Discuss what that means regarding the amounts that all the school families threw away. Ask the kids where they think all the trash goes.

MATERIALS:

- "Recycling Record" sheet (see page 117)
- large butcher paper

Consider This

Keep track of the weight of your classroom recycling box each week. Challenge the kids to help cut down on the amount of paper that goes into the box by using scraps and the backs of papers.

RECYCLING RECORD

Over the next _____ days, count the number of items thrown out at your house and write the numbers below. Bring the sheet back to school on _____.
                  (date)

Number of tin cans _____

Number of aluminum cans _____

Number of glass bottles, jars, and other glass containers _____

Number of plastic jugs, bottles, and other plastic containers _____

Number of plastic bags _____

Number of magazines/catalogs _____

Number of bundles of newspapers _____

Make a Difference

MATERIALS:
• letter (see below)

Have each child take a copy of the letter home to her parents or another family member. When the children bring in the requested items from home, have them sort them into the correct storage bins in your classroom. Let the children decorate the storage bins and make things from the items (for example, rain sticks [see page 51] or binoculars from toilet paper or paper towel rolls). Eventually, take a picture for the classroom newsletter showing how the class used the items that they brought in and recycled.

Dear Parents,

We need your help! Each day people throw things in the trash that we could be using at school. Here is a list of things that we could recycle and utilize in our learning. Please help by sending in the following items:

coffee tins	**egg cartons**	**film containers**	**frosting containers**
newspapers	**magazines**	**detergent tops**	**toilet/paper towel rolls**

Thanks for helping us to help our planet!

_____
Student's Name

_____
Teacher's Name and Grade Level

Trash in the Can

Discuss with the children the meaning of the saying "One man's garbage is another man's treasure." Explain that we may save or cherish things that others think we should throw away, and also that others may cherish things that we think they should throw away. Ask each child to name something that she can't bear to part with and that she considers a "real treasure." Explain that these items are often stored in the garage or attic and are things whose value others can't see, such as an old pair of comfortable shoes, a favorite worn-out cap, clothes that don't fit, a favorite stuffed animal, and so forth. Tell each child to draw on the garbage can a picture of what she thought of and to decorate the can as a "Treasure Can."

MATERIALS:
- "Garbage Can" reproducible (see page 120)
- ribbon
- gems, glitter, and/or stickers
- stamps

Happy/Sad Earth

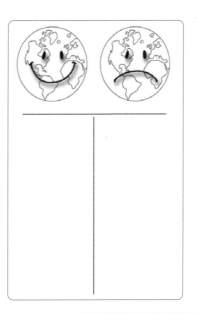

Talk with the children about what we do that pollutes the Earth and what we can do to keep the Earth clean. Ask them to fill in the columns of their sheets by either drawing or writing things that make the Earth happy and things that make the Earth sad.

MATERIALS:
- "Earth" reproducible (see page 121)

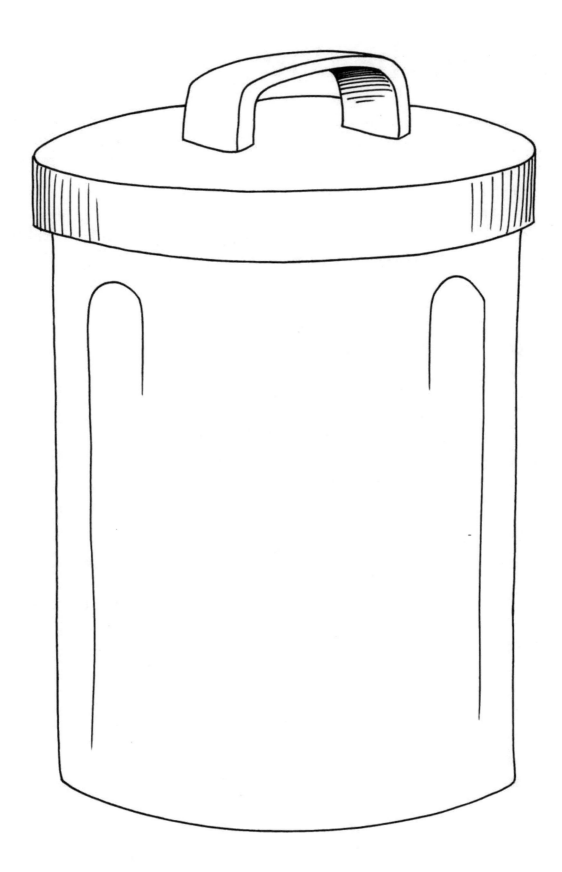

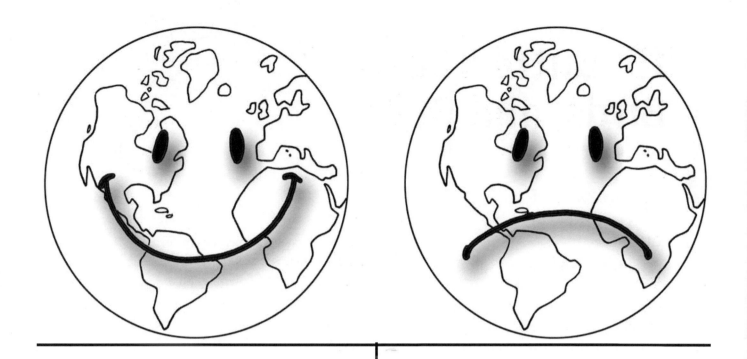

15. Butterflies, Birds, and Bees

Tune: "Buffalo Gals"

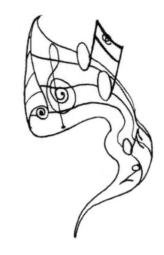

CHORUS:

Butterflies, birds, and bees can fly,
   way up high, in the sky.
Up in the sky, they can fly so high,
Butterflies, birds, and bees.

Butterfly, fly, won't you fly me away?
   Fly me away? Fly me away?
Butterfly, fly, won't you fly me away?
Fly me away to the moon.

Bumblebee, buzz, don't you buzz my ear,
   buzz my ear, buzz my ear.
Bumblebee, buzz, don't you buzz my ear.
Bumblebee, buzz away.

CHORUS

Hummingbird, flap, can you flap your wings?
   Flap your wings? Flap your wings?
Hummingbird, flap, can you flap your wings?
Fly all the way to the moon.

Dragonfly, fly, on a summer's day.
   a summer's day, a summer's day.
Dragonfly, fly, on a summer's day.
Dragonfly, fly away.

CHORUS

Ladybug crawling down my nose,
   down my nose, down my nose.
Ladybug crawling down my nose.
Ladybug, fly away!

Crickets at night play a noisy tune,
   a noisy tune, a noisy tune.
Crickets at night play a noisy tune,
A song they love to play.

CHORUS

All you mosquitoes annoying me,
   annoying me, annoying me.
All you mosquitoes annoying me,
Please go away!

Seven ants busy building a farm,
   building a farm, building a farm.
Seven ants busy building a farm,
A farm they built for you.

CHORUS repeats 3 times

Hide a Bug

Have the children visit the library and check out books on a variety of bugs. Give each child two slips of paper, and tell the children to each pick one bug, write a fact about it on one slip of paper, and draw a picture of it on the other slip. Use a permanent marker to number the plastic eggs and have each child fold up her drawing and place it in one of the plastic eggs. Hang or display the fact slips. Ask each child to choose an egg and to match the picture inside to one of the fact slips. Write the correct number on the back with a pencil. You can make this activity easier by assigning bugs to children and using a limited number of eggs for guessing.

MATERIALS:

- any number of plastic eggs
- slips of paper that will fit inside the eggs
- permanent marker

#2 FACT: . . .

#2

What Bugs You?

This activity provides a wonderful catalyst for getting kids to talk about things that bug them. It's not only fun to do, but it also makes a good "springboard" for a discussion of how to handle some of life's annoyances. Just writing them down or talking about them seems to help the kids "let go." Begin by asking the children to think about things that "bug them." Model a few that annoy you too, such as messy hair, mean people, mosquitoes, litterbugs, weird sounds, cold coffee, flat pillows, and so on. Have the children draw or write what bugs them on their suitcases so that they can pack them up and "send them away."

MATERIALS:

- "Suitcase" reproducible (see page 124)

What bugs you?

Messy hair

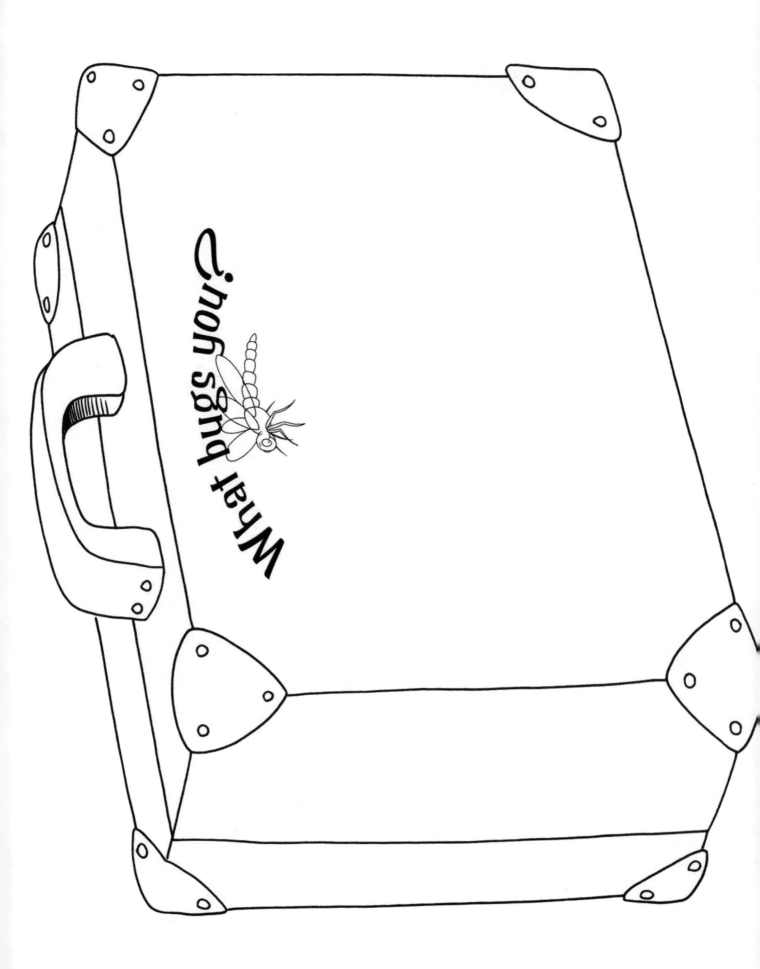

Bug Simile

Discuss with your class what a simile is and write some examples on the blackboard. Tell the children that it is sometimes easier to describe something by comparing it to something else, and that a simile is a comparison that often uses the word *like* or *as*. For example, "It tastes like dirt" will probably conjure up a thought of something you don't want to try—even if you haven't tasted dirt before. Comparing something to dirt makes you realize that it probably wouldn't taste good. Ask each child to investigate a bug that the class may not be familiar with and to fill in the reproducible form to describe that bug, using more familiar terms.

MATERIALS:
• "Simile Form" (below)

SIMILE FORM

_____ is like a _____.

It gets around like a _____.

It is the same color as a _____.

It reminds me of _____.

I like them as much as I like _____.

It is smaller than a _____ and bigger

than a _____.

I Wish I Were a Butterfly

MATERIALS:

- film container with slit cut in the side, 1 for each child
- *I Wish I Were a Butterfly* by James Howe
- life cycle of butterfly or "I Wish I Were a Butterfly" reproducible (see page 127)

Read the book aloud to your children, and then use this activity as a way for them to learn how to retell a story. Give each child a reproducible strip and a film container with a slit cut in the side, large enough to insert the strip. Ask the children to color their strips and then roll each one around a pencil so that the strips will fit inside the film containers. Show them how to roll a strip so that it can be pulled out of the container in the correct sequence. Have the children retell the story by sliding one bug at a time out of their containers. Then have them repeat the line that the butterfly says at the end of the story, but using the name of the bug that they have just pulled from the container, such as "Boy, I wish I were a cricket," or "Boy, I wish I were a glow worm," and so forth. I recommend using *I Wish I Were a Butterfly* because it sends home the message that whereas we all can see great things in other people, those other people may also see great things in us.

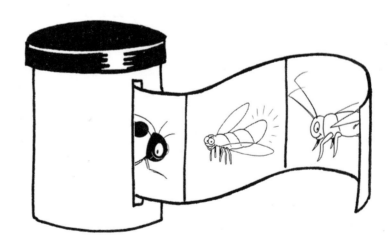

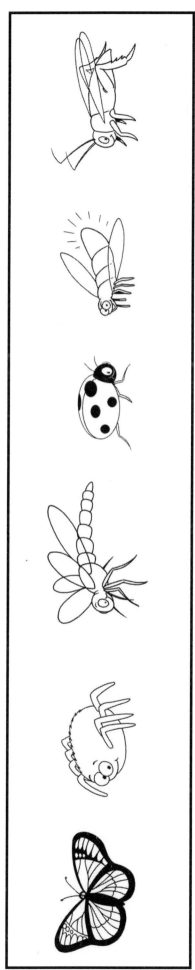
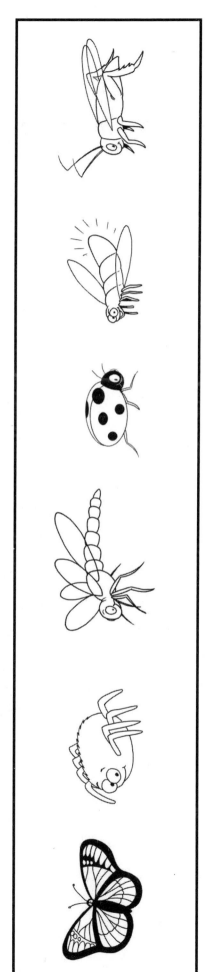
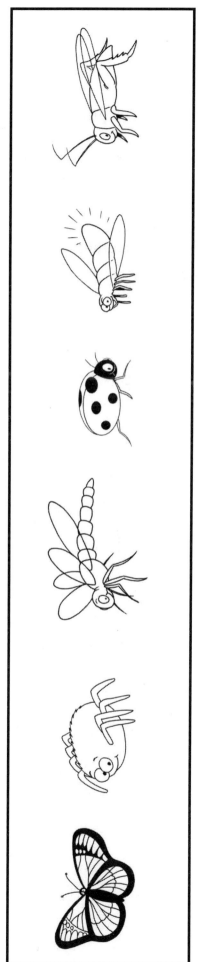

For other products by Donna Whyte, contact Crystal Springs Books at 1-800-321-0401, or visit our Web site at www.crystalsprings.com

Sing Yourself Smart Activity Book #7660

Sing Yourself Smart – CD #7112

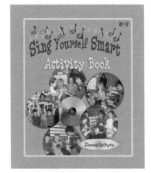

Read with Your Smartie # 7659

131 Ways to Use Film Containers:
   To Teach Literacy, Math, and Science–
   and Just to Have Fun! #8211

Dinosaurs, Popcorn, Penguins
& More – CD #8296